Prosperity Guaranteed

Prosperity Guaranteed

Universal Spiritual Principles That Bring Peace, Joy and Abundance

Grace Terry, MSW

Lucky Press, LLC ~ Lancaster, Ohio

Note: Many words of wisdom have been forwarded to the author and while credit is given whenever authorship is known, at times the originator can only be designated as "Author Unknown." We acknowledge the contributions of these unknown authors and will gladly update future editions, should authorship become established.

Published by:
Lucky Press, LLC
www.luckypress.com/prosperityguaranteed

PRINTED IN THE UNITED STATES OF AMERICA

ISBN: 0-9706377-8-0
LIBRARY OF CONGRESS CONTROL NUMBER: 2001098668

This book is dedicated to

Jim Auxier,

my beloved husband, lover,

prosperity partner,

master teacher, most gifted student,

friend, companion, soul-mate.

With your partnership, I experience prosperity

I otherwise might never have known.

Disclaimer

This publication is designed to provide competent and reliable information regarding the subject matter covered. However, it is sold with the understanding that the author and publisher are not engaged in rendering financial, legal, psychotherapeutic, medical, or other professional advice. If expert assistance is required, the services of a competent professional should be sought.

Every effort has been made to make this workbook as accurate as possible. However, there may be mistakes, both typographical and in content. Therefore, this text should be used only as a general guide and not as the ultimate source of information or direction. The ultimate source of information and direction is found within each reader.

The purpose of this workbook is to educate, to motivate, and to inspire. In the event you use any of the information in this book for yourself, which is your constitutional right, the author and the publisher assume no responsibility for your actions.

Table of Contents

Table of Contents

Acknowledgments

Most of the ideas and concepts of this book are not original. This is my interpretation of and experience with universal spiritual principles that have been taught by countless teachers through the ages. The possible exception may be the "51 percent rule" mentioned in several chapters. I have never seen or heard this particular concept written or taught by other teachers, but certainly there could be others sharing this principle without my knowledge.

Also, the definition of prosperity used in this workbook is original. It has evolved with input from many workshop participants over the years.

By far the most significant teacher I have had in learning spiritual principles of prosperity is Edwene Gaines. You can visit her web-site at www.prosperityproducts.com, write to her at P.O. Box 125, Valley Head, AL 35989 or send her e-mail to prosper@peop.tds.net. Edwene's tape set titled "Prosperity Plus," the one that literally changed my life, is still available along with other transformational products.

I must also acknowledge my gratitude to my dear friend and spiritual sister, Brenda Joyce Garner, who first introduced me to Edwene's ministry.

Other spiritual teachers who have been very influential in my life include Shakti Gawain, Louise Hay, John Bradshaw, and Harville Hendrix. I highly recommend these teachers and their publications to you.

I am grateful to the Revs. Richard and Judy Thomas at Unity of Louisville (Kentucky), to the Rev. David Leonard at the Huntsville (Alabama) Church of Religious Science, and to the Rev. Ed Dilworth of the Louisiana Conference of the United Methodist Church, for their trust, friendship, support, and guidance through the years.

My heartfelt thanks go to my good friend Sue Cummings, whose editorial assistance has contributed immensely to the quality of this effort.

Certainly I must acknowledge my husband, Jim Auxier, who has supported me and encouraged me unfailingly during the creation of this workbook. This project is a "leap of faith" for him as for me.

Perhaps most important, I am grateful to the many clients and workshop participants who have shared their journeys with me over the years. I have never taught a workshop without learning. I have never given my energy and attention to a client without gaining insight and wisdom. Teaching prosperity has helped me to learn, re-learn, and integrate these principles. My students have truly been my teachers.

Introduction

How can prosperity be guaranteed?

Here's how. This is a workbook. Go through the book and complete the suggested assignments to the best of your ability. Recruit at least one "prosperity partner" to support you and to share this adventure with you. Keep a journal, documenting your process. If after giving the project your best effort you are not completely satisfied with the results, return the book and a copy of your journal to me for a full refund on the workbook. No tricks. No hassles. No kidding.

How can an author be so confident of her material?

It's simple. I've been practicing these principles for many years and they have worked for me, bringing me peace and prosperity beyond anything I could have imagined when I began this journey. I've also been teaching these principles in workshops for many years and my students have testified to the power and effectiveness of these principles. I know the Universe does not play favorites. The principles I teach in this book are UNIVERSAL spiritual principles. Universal means they work every time for every one who uses them — just like physical laws.

Think about the physical law of gravity. How often does gravity work? Ask any parent of a high-chair baby who has repeatedly retrieved the spoon after the precious little one has gleefully tossed in onto the floor over and over. Gravity works 100 percent of the time. The spiritual principles, or laws, that create prosperity are just as reliable. I am so confident of this that I am willing to guarantee the results of my book.

Universal also means that the principles are at work ALL THE TIME, whether we are conscious of them or not. By being conscious of the principles and mindfully using them, we can work with them to create the life we want. **My purpose in writing this book is to help you become aware of and use universal spiritual principles in such a way that you create a prosperous, joyful life that is a blessing not only to you but to others as well.**

If you bought this workbook, I assume you are ready to make significant changes in your life — one step at a time. Using this workbook can be a pivotal event in your personal journey if you are ready and willing to follow suggestions and do the footwork.

I celebrate and applaud your commitment and courage. I support you 100 percent with no conditions.

My Story

I want to share with you some things about my family and personal life in order for you to fully appreciate what these principles have accomplished for me.

Born in 1954, I grew up in a working class family in a small paper mill town (population 17,000) in the rural deep South. Like 90 percent of the fathers in our little town, my dad worked at the paper mill. Like 90 percent of the mothers, my mom did not work outside the home. We lived in a small three-bedroom, one-bath frame house in a neighborhood of similar homes.

My parents lived paycheck to paycheck and often argued about money. As an adult, I realize this was just one concrete, tangible way that my mom and dad addressed deeper, more abstract conflicts in their relationship.

As a child, I internalized my parents' anxiety and conflict about money. Unconsciously, I came to believe in scarcity, the idea that there is not enough to go around and that if I enjoyed any material thing somehow I was taking something away from someone else who deserved it more than I. I felt like a burden to my parents. I did not feel worthy of enjoying the good things that life offered me.

My early religious experiences only added to my feelings of guilt and shame. Like most of the families in our community, my family attended a fundamentalist church that constantly emphasized sin, human depravity, and damnation. The most commonly quoted Scripture was an obscure passage from the Old Testament which stated, "all our righteousnesses are as filthy rags in the eyes of the Lord" (Isaiah 64:6).

I decided early in life to pursue education and career in order to create a different kind of life from the one my parents lived. As a college student I rejected the church as ridiculously outdated, irrelevant and sexist. I chose the field of psychotherapy for my profession. As a participant in human potential encounter groups I had "peak experiences," transcendent moments of profound joy and connectedness. I came to believe that psychotherapy was the only hope that I and others like me had for healing hidden wounds of childhood and living a joyful life.

I completed college and graduate school after eight years of determined struggle. I launched my career as a psychotherapist as I continued to pursue my own personal healing and growth. I married and divorced. Bitter and cynical after the divorce, I became agnostic — doubting the existence of anything that made sense in this absurd, chaotic world. I saw myself as a helpless victim, totally at the mercy of capricious fate.

Married or single, I struggled financially. Even with a professional degree, licenses, and credentials, I managed to set myself up to be always overworked, underpaid, and anxious about money — not surprisingly, *just like my parents.*

Just a few years out of graduate school I took a position as a counselor in an addiction treatment center. While I had never had problems with alcohol or other drugs, I soon realized that I displayed all of the symptoms of addiction. My drugs of choice were food (particularly sugar and refined carbohydrates), work, and dysfunctional relationships. Desperate and miserable, I became involved in a twelve-step recovery group. It was here I was first taught the difference between religion and spirituality. Rather than rigid religious dogma, I was introduced for the first time to the idea of a Higher Power that I could choose — a Higher Power that fit my needs and worked for me.

I will be forever grateful for the many gifts I received from twelve-step fellowships. First and foremost, I was relieved of my shame-based compulsion to self-destruct.

Looking past the sexist language of the "Big Book" of *Alcoholics Anonymous*, I read such liberating passages as this on page 46:

"...we did not need to consider another's conception of God. Our own conception, however inadequate, was sufficient to make the approach and to effect a contact with (God). As soon as we admitted the possible existence of a Creative Intelligence, a Spirit of the Universe underlying the totality of things, we began to be possessed of a new sense of power and direction. ... We found that God does not make too hard terms with those who seek (God). To us, the Realm of Spirit is broad, roomy, all inclusive; never exclusive or forbidding to those who earnestly seek. It is open, we believe to all ..."

Other passages in the same chapter of the book refer to God as an:

"All Powerful, Guiding, Creative Intelligence," the "Spirit of the Universe," and the "Presence of Infinite Power and Love."

And how about this for a shocker — (page 133):

"We are sure God wants us to be happy, joyous, and free."

And this on page 55:

"We found the Great Reality deep down within us. In the last analysis it is only here that (God) may be found."

I highly recommend AA's "Big Book" to any seeker of Truth — whether or not that person has ever struggled with alcohol, other drugs, or other addictions. I particularly recommend Chapter 4 — *"We Agnostics."*

My experiences in twelve-step recovery constituted a major turning point for me, personally, professionally, and spiritually. Through a twelve-step group for adult children of dysfunctional families, I met a radiant, charismatic woman who became a close friend. She was a student and teacher of Truth. One day she offered to loan me a tape set on prosperity. I gratefully accepted.

The tape set was entitled *Prosperity Plus* by Edwene Gaines. In this audio recording of a prosperity workshop taught by Edwene, I was first introduced to the revolutionary idea that the Creator of the Universe wants me to have everything I need, that there is a divine purpose for my life that includes joy and abundance, and that if I follow certain simple spiritual principles, then all my needs will be provided for. Edwene also introduced me to a Bible that is FULL of prosperity promises.

At one point in the workshop Edwene stated emphatically, "I serve God. Money serves me." I was thunderstruck! In my twelve-step recovery I had been led through step three in which I made a decision to "turn my will and my life over to the care of God as I understood (God)." I had taken this step as honestly and sincerely and completely as I knew how at the time. But when I heard Edwene say "I serve God. Money serves me." I became aware that, truly, I had only turned my addictions over to the care of God. I could not honestly say my life was about serving God. I was still rather self-centered and self-absorbed.

At that point, I made a profound decision to surrender my will and my entire life to the care of my loving Higher Power, to serve the Universe to the best of my ability one day at a time, and to practice the spiritual principles of prosperity that were taught by Edwene Gaines in her transformational workshop.

That was in 1987. Later I was fortunate to have the opportunity to attend several workshops and retreats presented by Edwene. In the fall of 1988 I completed Master Prosperity Teacher Training with Edwene and her husband (at that time), Bert Carson. I was also fortunate to discover some other excellent teachers of prosperity.

As I studied and practiced these spiritual principles, my life radically changed. For the first time in my life, I was freed from fears and anxieties about money. As I became clear about what I wanted in my life, I manifested prosperity and abundance. I realized my long-held dream of creating a successful private psychotherapy practice. I was given the opportunity and the privilege of helping many others in their journey toward healing and light. And I prospered financially by doing so. I bought the home, the furniture, the car, the clothes and the jewelry I wanted.

Then I decided that, more than anything else, I wanted a spiritual partnership so that I could share all of the good things in my life. Adapting the same spiritual principles, I attracted my ideal life partner. We were married in 1994.

At this writing my husband and I are embarked on a grand adventure. We live, work, and travel full-time in our beautiful recreational vehicle (RV). Together we continue to practice and teach the principles of prosperity and we continue to learn and re-learn the fundamentals. Together we manifest prosperity and abundance that I might never have realized alone.

In the 1990's I started teaching prosperity workshops. By this time, the principles were working so magnificently for me that I felt compelled to share them. This workbook grew out of those workshops. My goal is to share my experiences and understanding with others, so that everyone might enjoy the rewards of prosperity consciousness. My goal is to continue to learn and to evolve in my understanding of spiritual truth. I am grateful that the Universe is a patient Teacher.

I am now very grateful to my parents and to all of the influences of my childhood. They provided the perfect school for me to learn some very important lessons.

I now realize that I have always been wealthy. Even when I was a child in that Southern paper mill town, even when I was a university student living hand to mouth for eight years, even when I created financial struggles for myself as a young professional, I had access to tremendous wealth. I have always had all I needed and enough to share. I am truly blessed.

Prosperity:

The continuous process of joyfully

receiving an abundance

of everything we need

and

joyfully giving back

from the overflow.

The Challenge of Language

Clarification of Key Concepts

For the purposes of this workbook, **I define prosperity as a continuous process of joyfully receiving an abundance of everything we need AND joyfully giving back from the overflow.**

What we need includes, and is not limited to, the following:

1) Physical needs: clean air, water, food, shelter, clothing, (in our economy, these usually require money or some other means of exchange), freedom from disease, discomfort, pain (may also require money), plenty of energy, vitality, and stamina.

2) Emotional/spiritual needs: self-esteem, esteem from others, love/affection, a dependable supply of "positive strokes" (i.e., recognition, affirmation, validation), a sense of belonging and connection, meaningful work, a sense of purpose and meaning.

This definition has evolved with the help of many workshop participants and spiritual teachers. Workshop participants — folks just like you — universally agree that if they were experiencing a continuous process of joyfully receiving all that they need (physically, emotionally, and spiritually) and joyfully giving back from the overflow, they would consider themselves sublimely prosperous.

Spirituality/religion — Perhaps some of you are uncomfortable with my discussion of spiritual principles. It is my belief that we are all spiritual beings, living in a spiritual universe, governed by spiritual law. **We are not human beings on a spiritual journey, but spiritual beings on a human journey.** Whether or not you believe this, these principles can still work for you.

You may be a religious person. If you are, and you are comfortable with your religious life, GREAT! If not, you do not have to become religious for these principles to work.

You do not have to have any faith in these principles for them to work. Does a person have to believe in gravity for gravity to work in their life? Of course not. Gravity works independently of an individual's belief or faith in gravity. The spiritual principles that attract and create prosperity work whether the individual believes they will work or not. You may find it necessary to change the way you think — about life, about yourself, about the Universe that you live in. You may have to *act as if* you believe some things even if you don't. (More about this later.) Be assured that my purpose is not to convert you to any particular religious creed or dogma. **My purpose is to increase your awareness of the unlimited possibilities available to you as a conscious Co-creator of your own life.**

While religion and spirituality are certainly not mutually exclusive, there is a difference. If this is a new concept for you, then this could be your first major lesson from using this book.

We probably all know people who are very religious who have very little conscious awareness of their own innate spirituality (inherent worth, value, preciousness, divinity) or the innate spirituality of others. You also may know spiritually conscious people who radiate joy, serenity, faith and unconditional love who do not have any formal religious affiliation. (If you do not know any people like this, trust me — they do exist!)

Then there are those people who participate in organized religious groups and activities AND whose lives are clearly governed by spiritual principles such as honesty, justice, surrender, faith, humility, courage, forgiveness, perseverance, commitment to service, and unconditional love. Mother Teresa, Mohandas Gandhi. and the Dalai Lama are all excellent examples. Rosalyn and Jimmy Carter also come to mind.

In my perception, humans are innately spiritual; that is, humans are innately creative, intuitive, loving, lovable, peaceful, and divine. Our secular culture (which includes patriarchal, shame-based religion) has repressed and distorted these innate human qualities in many if not most of us. The good news is that the Truth about us humans has not and can not be destroyed. Our essential spiritual nature has survived through eons of repression and is always there, ready to be called forth and revealed.

God/Godde/Spirit/etc. — when referring to the loving, creative force for good in the Universe, I usually use words like "Spirit" or "Higher Power" or "the Presence." When it seems that no other word will do I use the word "Godde." This is actually an Old English spelling of our modern English word "God." I prefer the Old English spelling in order to differentiate my meaning from the connotations commonly associated in our culture with the word God.

In the dominant Western culture, the word God too often evokes images of a male deity, somewhere "up there" and "out there," who is judging, keeping score, punishing, occasionally and randomly granting wishes to his favorites like a great cosmic slot machine. When I use the word Godde (or Spirit or Presence or other similar wording) I am referring to the Ultimate Unnamable Mystery, the universal creative Force for good, for health, for abundance, for love that is present in all of Creation.

This Force permeates and gives life to the physical world and at the same time transcends the physical world. It is thus perceived as meta-physical (i.e., beyond the physical) or spiritual.

This Force transcends our concepts of gender. If it is masculine it is also feminine — both and neither. In my personal prayer and meditation practices, if I am feeling a need to personify this Force, I visualize a holy family — a masculine father figure, a feminine mother figure, and a divine child. And I visualize all of this divine energy within me and within all of creation.

You may have more traditional concepts of God (for example, God as Heavenly Father, Savior or Lord). If so, this workbook still can be very useful to you. You may be atheist or agnostic. If so, the principles I share in this workbook can work for you.

If some of my spiritual ideas disagree with your concepts of reality, just set that aside for now and please keep an open mind. Again, you do not have to agree with my thinking on every point in order for this book to be helpful to you. It is not my goal to convert the readers of this book to my way of thinking. Throughout this book, I invite you to take what works for you and leave the rest.

Whatever your concepts (or lack of concepts) of God/Godde/the Force/Higher Power/the Great Spirit/etc., my question for you is this, "Is it working for you?"

I once saw a cartoon in the *Grapevine*, a monthly publication of Alcoholics Anonymous. In the cartoon a derelict, a shabby bum, sat on a park bench holding a tin cup, begging for money. Beside him was a sign that read, "I did it my way."

Do your concepts/ideas about life, about who you are and your place in the Universe, and about Godde create what you want in your life? If not, then you may want to consider modifying or adjusting your concepts to something that works more effectively for you. Deciding to change some of your ideas does not make you or the old ideas wrong. Deciding to change simply means you are on an evolutionary journey, willing to grow and to learn as more light is revealed.

One of my spiritual teachers once said to me, **"If you want what I have, do what I do."** I lovingly extend to you the same invitation.

How To Use This Workbook

The ideal way to use this workbook is with a small group of prosperity partners — from four to six people who will covenant together to regularly spend time writing in the workbook, writing in their journal, and meeting together to share with and support one another toward the goal of greater prosperity.

In order for the guarantee to be in effect, the user of this workbook must have at least one prosperity partner with whom to share this process. It can be a friend, a family member *other than your spouse or romantic partner,* a business associate, an Internet pal — anyone who will agree to purchase and complete their own workbook, keep their own journal, and talk with you regularly (at least three times a month, preferably once a week) about the process.

Why this stipulation? The reason is this: My own personal experience as a seeker and my experience as a teacher and healer tell me that we humans will do things with support and accountability that we will never do alone. I want you to have the support you need when you feel discouraged and want to give up. I want you to be willing to hold yourself accountable to at least one other person. I want you to experience the joy and power of spiritual partnership.

If you work with a small group, your group members can decide when and how often to meet. You can agree together that each of you will make your group meeting a priority — that each of you will commit to attending unless there is an unavoidable conflict or serious illness. You can agree to give one another unconditional acceptance and support. You can agree that whatever is shared within the group will remain confidential. (See Appendix 1 for more suggestions for your prosperity partners meeting.)

You might ask, "What if I find a partner and start working with them and then they quit?" Then you would, hopefully, bless them, release them, and find another partner and continue your adventure.

Remember — in having and being a partner, the objective is to serve as a witness and a companion for one another. In agreeing to be prosperity partners, you agree to be accountable *to* one another, but you are never responsible *for* one another. Each person is responsible for his/her own progress. There is no need for rescuers in this process.

You will notice that certain exercises in the workbook are marked with a heart, as in ♥. These exercises are lovingly REQUIRED if you are to take advantage of the money-back guarantee that comes with this workbook. That is, I can only guarantee the results of this workbook if you are willing to do the exercises marked with a ♥.

As you proceed through the workbook, I suggest you take each lesson in order. Write *something* in each lesson before proceeding to the next. Later on, if you wish, you can always come back and write more as your awareness grows.

Along with chapters one through six in the workbook are journal-writing assignments. Your journal can be any kind of loose-leaf or spiral notebook. It even can be a yellow legal pad, but a loose-leaf binder with tabs or a six-subject spiral notebook seems to work better. If you use a six-subject notebook, start a new section of the notebook with each chapter.

Keep your workbook and your journal in a safe place. If you have to, keep it in a locked briefcase. Do whatever you have to do to protect your privacy and to feel at ease about writing down whatever you need to write. As you complete your writing assignments, know that you will not be required to share every word with your partner(s).

Take as much time as you need to complete this workbook. A few will complete the process in six months. Most will need nine months, a year, or more. As you work through the lessons you will realize that they all overlap and support one another in a circular fashion. The principles all work together harmoniously to bring about miraculous results. I guarantee it.

The important thing is to spend some time (ideally an hour or more) at least once a week writing in the workbook and journal and regularly sharing with your partner(s).

At the end of each chapter I have included some material from the prosperity scrapbook that I have been creating for many years — stories, quotes, and poems. I also have included some affirmations that may be useful to you. You can create your own affirmations if you wish — these are some that have been helpful to me.

For each chapter I also have included Bible verses that are meaningful to me in my study and practice of prosperity principles. For each principle I have tried to include some Scripture passages from Hebrew Scripture (the Old Testament), from the gospels (the life and teachings of Jesus of Nazareth, the carpenter rabbi), and from later New Testament writers.

If in the past well-meaning teachers have used the Bible to shame and/or abuse you, I invite you to open your heart to the Divine Love contained in these words. (I also invite you to overlook/transcend the sexist language!) Also, remember as you read that the Divine Being mentioned in the Scriptures is inside you — a part of you! — not just out there somewhere.

Of course, if you choose, you can just ignore and overlook the Scripture references. These spiritual principles for creating prosperity will work with or without the Biblical references. However, I would venture to say that almost any educated, open-minded person would agree that the Bible contains universal spiritual wisdom which can benefit any student of Truth.

The Scripture references I include are just a sampling of the prosperity principles contained in the Bible. I would encourage anyone to further study the sacred scriptures of all the great faiths in order to fully enjoy the richness and wisdom contained there.

There may be a time when you are working on an exercise and are asked to answer a question or fill in a sentence, and you go completely blank. To your conscious mind at that moment, you have not the foggiest clue as to what the truth might be. Do not fret or worry. Just make up something! Really! Act as if you know the Truth and just write whatever comes to mind. It may seem sheer fantasy at the time you are writing, but that's OK. Acting as if you know the Truth will lead you to the Truth! I guarantee it! **There is a part of you that knows everything you need to know.** Trust that part of you to lead you into complete awareness, healing, and abundant prosperity.

There may be times when the suggestions in the workbook seem difficult, unreasonable, or painful. Be assured that I have not asked you to do ANYTHING in this process that I have not done myself — over and over — with good results.

If at any time during the process you experience painful awareness, this is nothing to fear. Rejoice! Yes, rejoice! The pain was already there, outside of your conscious awareness. If it were bad enough to kill you, you would already be dead! The pain is now coming to your conscious awareness to be released and healed. Just notice without judging this process. Breathe, write about it, and talk about it with your prosperity partner(s). If you are inclined to prayer, pray about it. As you breathe, write, talk, and/or pray, release the pain. Just let it go.

At any point you are free to decide whether or not you will continue the process, whether or not you will be thoroughly honest with yourself and/or your partner(s), whether or not you complete all of the assignments. However, if you wish to realize the guaranteed results, then you will just do it.

If you reach a point where you are highly resistant to continuing, write in your journal about your resistance. Are there fears about moving forward? What's the worst thing that could happen? Be gentle and accepting of yourself as you face these fears and walk through them. Remember, **courage is NOT the absence of fear, but action in spite of fear.**

As you embark on this adventure, know that **your best is good enough.** If you are honestly giving this project your best effort, **you cannot do it wrong.** The results of your work will speak for themselves. Do not judge, grade, or second-guess yourself.

Above all, have FUN with this process! For me, an important aspect of prosperity is enjoying life at every point in the experience. Practice finding the joy along the way.

Again,…
- I applaud you,
- I celebrate you,
- I support you 100 percent without condition.

The ENTIRE UNIVERSE…
- applauds you,
- celebrates you,
- supports you 100 percent without condition.

You are a winner! Failure is impossible.

Chapter 1: The Power of Your Thoughts and Beliefs

"You are given the gifts of the gods; you create your reality according to your beliefs. There are no limitations to the self, except those you believe in."
—Jane Roberts

In learning to manifest prosperity in my life one of the first things I had to do was to become aware of and then change my thinking, particularly my thinking about myself, about the nature of Godde, and about life and the universe in general. For instance, I became aware I had a deeply held belief that life is a struggle. That thinking — that belief — became a self-fulfilling prophecy. Believing that life is a struggle, I ingeniously managed to create constant struggle for myself - even at times when struggle was not necessary!

Now I choose to believe **"Life is a joyful adventure, full of rich opportunities and pleasures for me to enjoy!"** And that belief becomes a self-fulfilling prophecy. Consciously choosing this belief, I now create a life full of adventure, rich opportunities, and pleasures to enjoy!

To build prosperity consciousness it is important to CONSTANTLY be aware of and monitor what you are thinking — what you are believing — what you are telling yourself to be true. As you become more and more aware, you can stop yourself from affirming shame, guilt, scarcity, or poverty in your world. **Whenever you hear yourself thinking negative, blaming, judging, critical (of self or others), victim thoughts — you can immediately replace those with loving, forgiving, life-affirming, self-esteem building, abundance-consciousness thoughts. This is the energy of prosperity! Positive results will follow immediately.**

Most of us are not even aware of what we think. Our minds are so miraculous — we think our thoughts so quickly and automatically — that the whole process typically occurs on an unconscious or pre-conscious level. I prefer to use the term pre-conscious because it implies that the process can be brought into the conscious realm. We just need to tune in and listen to ourselves.

"I know men and women can banish worry, fear and various kinds of illnesses, and can transform their lives by changing their thoughts. I know! I know! I know! I have seen such incredible transformations performed hundreds of times. I have seen them so often that I no longer wonder at them."

—From the writings of Dale Carnegie

"The thing always happens that you really believe in and the belief in the thing makes it happen."
— Frank Lloyd Wright

We also need to be conscious of the words we say, which are a reflection of our thoughts and beliefs, and to make sure our words are those that will create and attract prosperity.

Whatever we think — whatever we tell ourselves is true — will be true in our universe. If we believe in scarcity and think thoughts of scarcity we will create scarcity and lack. If we think thoughts of abundance and prosperity, we will create abundance and prosperity.

Some of you are thinking, "But it's not that simple." It is absolutely that simple. I guarantee it. I guarantee that if you begin to consistently think positive thoughts of prosperity and abundance and speak words of prosperity and abundance you will begin to attract and create more prosperity and abundance in your life.

You may be wondering, "Do I have to think and speak positive thoughts 100 percent of the time before I can enjoy prosperity?" The answer is no.

I have noticed something in my own journey and in the journeys of countless others who have shared with me. There seems to be a principle at work that I call the "51 percent rule." The way it works is this: When we get 51 percent healed, tremendous things start happening. We still have more healing work to do, but while we're doing it the windows of heaven start to open up and pour blessings down on us.

So when 51 percent of our thoughts, beliefs, and words affirm prosperity, we begin to enjoy overflowing abundance and prosperity!

Our willingness and sheer determination and the support of our partners gets us to the 51 percent point. After that, we still need willingness and determination and support to get us the rest of the way, but we already are enjoying the rich rewards of our work.

Trust me on this. Try it to see if you do not find this to be true in your journey. Just be sure to hang in there until you get to the 51 percent mark! There is no way, really, to know when you are approaching that point. But just think, if you give up and quit, you could very well be quitting at the 49 percent point. As they say in twelve-step programs, "Don't leave until you get your miracle!"

Like me, you may have been programmed early in life to think negative, shame-based thoughts: for example, "I don't deserve to be happy." The good news is this: As a conscious adult, you can decide what you think! You can re-program your thinking any way you want! Like me, you can bless and thank and release your early teachers. They gave you the perfect opportunity to learn how to transcend early programming and create something new for yourself. You can re-decide for yourself what you think without making anyone wrong.

The choice is yours! *Lack of awareness is the same as having no choice.* With conscious awareness, we have choices! We can choose the thoughts and words of poverty and victimhood (and continue to live with the consequences) or we can choose the thoughts and words that invite abundant prosperity.

So your first prosperity lesson is to decide what you think — about yourself, about life in general, and about the nature of the Divine. To those who have no belief in a Supreme/Ultimate/Infinite Power or Energy or Force, it is important that you are at peace with that decision. To those who do have a concept of Godde, it is important that your concept of Godde (the Divine, the Great Spirit) support your prosperity.

Do not underestimate the importance of this seemingly simple concept! If you want to know what you REALLY believe, look at your life. **Your life is a perfect mirror of your beliefs. YOU HAVE THE LIFE YOU BELIEVE YOU DESERVE.** If you are experiencing or perceiving ANY lack or scarcity or poverty in ANY area of your life, something about your thinking and/or your beliefs needs to change in order for you to experience abundant prosperity.

Also remember — **if you always do what you always did, you will always get what you always got!** If you want to get something different, it's time to DO something different!

Exercises

Awareness Exercise — a gentle reminder: You cannot do this wrong! There are no wrong answers. If you're not sure of the answer, make up something! Act as if you know the answer!

♥   Consider for a moment how your mother (or the most significant female caregiver of your childhood) might have completed the following statements. Write down what you think she might have said if she were being completely honest.

"Life _____"

"God _____"

"I am _____"

"Money _____"

♥   Consider how your father (or the most significant male caregiver of your childhood) might have completed the following statements. Write down what you think he might have said if he were being completely honest.

"Life _____"

"God_____"

"I am _____"

"Money_____"

It doesn't matter so much what they actually might have said. It matters what you <u>think</u> they would have said.

♥ **Journal writing assignment:** Write an entry answering this question: How have you been influenced by your parents' or caregivers' ideas about life, about Godde, about themselves, and about money. How would you like that to change? Share with your prosperity partners.

Shared on: ___/___/___(date).

♥ **To Do:** If you become aware that you may have learned some scarcity or poverty consciousness from your parents or other caregivers, stop now for a moment, close your eyes, relax, and breathe. Allow an image of these early teachers to form in your imagination. See yourself as grown-up and powerful and loving in relationship to them. Say to them something like, "Thank you for being my teacher. I bless you and release you. I now choose to live my life in accordance with my own beliefs." Or say whatever seems honest and loving. Let them go. Stay with the imagery until you feel complete for now. Gently open your eyes and stretch.

♥ **Journal writing assignment:** After you do this exercise, write about it in your journal and talk about it with your prosperity partner(s).

Discussed on: ____/____/____ (date).

If anything about this exercise was painful or uncomfortable for you, just make a mental (or literal) note of that for now. We will come back to that later in the chapter on forgiveness.

In order to experience abundant prosperity, we must be clear that we are worthy of and deserving of this good in our lives. Acting as if we are clear about our inherent worthiness, preciousness, and divinity will help us to get clear!

♥ Write down at least five positive statements (affirmations) about yourself. You do not have to believe every one of the statements wholeheartedly. Just write five positive statements you believe to be true or would like to believe to be true about you. (Hint: If you have difficulty completing this list, ask people who know you well to help you create five affirmations about yourself. It's not cheating to ask for help! You can also check the affirmations at the end of this chapter.)

1. _____

2. _____

3. _____

4. _____

5. _____

♥ After you have written your list, write the answer to this question: If I truly believed all these things were true about me, how would my life be different? How would my behavior be different? List at least three specific behaviors.

_____

_____

_____

_____

_____

♥ Now make this commitment: For the next 30 days (or whatever it takes), I am willing to ACT AS IF I believe I am worthy of love, abundance, and prosperity.

_____   ___/___/___

(signature)   (date)

Again, in order to experience prosperity and abundance, we must get clear that life and the Universe are engineered in such a way that prosperity and abundance are not only possible but unfailingly available to all who are willing to receive.

♥ Write down at least five positive statements (affirmations) about life or the Universe in general. Make sure these are statements that will increase your prosperity.

1. _____

2. _____

3. _____

4. _____

5. _____

♥   Now answer this question: If I truly believed all these positive things about life/the Universe, how would my life be different? How would my behavior be different? Write down at least three specific behaviors.

_____

_____

_____

_____

_____

♥   Now, make this commitment: For the next 30 days, or whatever it takes, I am willing to ACT AS IF I believe these positive things about life and the Universe.

_____   ___/___/___

(signature)   (date)

The following is ♥ (required) for those who choose to believe in God/Godde/a Higher Power/Great Spirit/etc. OR for anyone who is willing to act as if you believe on an experimental basis.

Imagine the Godde of this Universe is EVERYTHING you need and want it to be in order to bring you the prosperity you desire in your life. Write down all of the qualities and characteristics of this Godde. (Again, it's OK to get some help with this one if you need it.)

Qualities and characteristics of the Godde of my choosing:

_____

_____

_____

Now answer the following question: If I truly believed the Godde of this Universe had these qualities and characteristics, how would my life be different? How would my behavior be different? List at least three specific behaviors that would be different:

_____

_____

_____

Now make this commitment: For the next 30 days, or whatever it takes, I will ACT AS IF the Godde of this Universe is all of the things I need and want it to be in order for me to bring abundant prosperity into my life.

_____   ___/___/___
(signature)   (date)

♥ Discuss this process with your prosperity partner(s).

Discussed on: ___/___/___ (date).

♥ **Journal writing assignment:** Date and write an entry in your journal, recording anything you learned, relearned, or became aware of from doing this exercise (creating your affirmations, etc.)

Discuss with your prosperity partner(s).

Discussed on: ___/___/___ (date).

♥ **Journal writing assignment:** (The following is ♥ required for those who decide NOT to believe in a Higher Power/Divine Spirit/Godde.) Date an entry in your journal and write a paragraph or two about how you reached that decision. As you write, notice if there is any indication of anger or hurt in what you write.

Be sure to discuss this with your prosperity partner(s).

Discussed on: ___/___/___ (date).

If you detect any anger or hurt in your decision, remember this when we reach the chapter on forgiveness. Those who decide that they do not believe in a Higher Power can certainly enjoy prosperity. However, it is important for the decision to be made peacefully rather than from pain.

♥ **To Do:** On index cards, write down the five positive statements (affirmations) about yourself, about life/the Universe, and the qualities and characteristics of your Higher Power (if you chose to do that). Put the index cards in a place where you will see them every day — on your refrigerator, microwave, or computer screen, in your appointment book, or on your bathroom mirror. Make several sets if you wish and post them in more than one location. Take a few moments every day to read through these affirmations and to remind yourself that you are ACTING AS IF you believe these statements 100 percent!

Completed on: ___/___/___ (date).

To Do: The following is optional: Make a recording of these affirmations plus some others that are especially powerful for you. Listen to the recording as you dress each morning, in your car, as you exercise — whenever you can! You cannot hear the truth too often!

If you have come this far, CONGRATULATIONS! Give yourself a great big hug and a pat on the back! You are taking a giant step in consciousness. You are transforming/re-creating your world by the power of your thoughts — the most powerful force in your Universe!

Affirmations

I am a spiritual being on a human journey.

I am a spiritual being, living in a spiritual Universe, governed by spiritual law.

I love, honor, and nurture myself. I am lovable, valuable, and precious.

I am uniquely gifted and I joyfully share my gifts with the Universe.

I now discover how wonderful I am. I choose to love and enjoy myself.

The Universe is safe and friendly. I am safe. I am at peace.

I trust that right action is always taking place in my life. I am at peace.

I choose now to live in a world of peace, power, and prosperity.

I have a commitment to health, love, joy, wisdom, and abundance.

There is more than enough for every spiritual being to have all he or she desires.

There is more than enough love on planet Earth for everyone, including me!

The Universe loves me!

I am courageous and clear. I speak words of truth and power.

I am joyous, peaceful, healthy, enthusiastic, wise, loving, and rich right now!!

Within me is a source of infinite wisdom, love, and creativity. Whenever I need guidance, I go within and find the answers I need.

The entire Universe supports my dreams, ventures, and projects. There is plenty of time, space, and resources for everything I want to do.

Godde-in-me is my overflowing source of all good.

I am enriched and prospered all the time. The Universe provides!

Godde is lavish, unfailing Abundance, the rich omnipresent substance of the Universe.

My thoughts, words, and deeds create peace and prosperity for all.

I am one with all the good in the Universe.

I deserve love, joy, and prosperity.

I am a loving and lovable person. I deserve dignity and respect. I respect myself.

I appreciate my own uniqueness. I am a living, moving miracle.

I am open and willing to change.

I am learning to understand everyone and everything around me as my teacher.

I look at life optimistically, and I am eager to accept new challenges.

I am now willing to change, grow, risk, play, and love with passionate abandon.

It is safe to see and experience new ideas and new ways. I am open and receptive to good.

I rejoice in my own expression of life. I am perfect just as I am. I love and approve of myself.

I acknowledge and accept that I am the creative power in my world.

"I give thanks for the goodness of this day. I am in the midst of opportunities as great as anyone has ever known. All that I seek (perfect health, wealth, love and full self-expression) is seeking me. God's Power moves my thought into expression. I plan and act in confidence and the joy of living life successfully is mine."
— Dr. and Mrs. Alexander Mulligan

A special affirmation for women: It is safe for me to be a strong, smart, beautiful spiritual woman of power.

The following prayer treatments (affirmations) were transcribed from a tape entitled Overflowing Abundance, *by Dr. Frederick Eikerenkoetter, affectionately known as Rev. Ike.*

Overflowing Abundance

God-in-me is my overflowing supply of all good. I thank and praise God-in-me for my overflowing source of health, happiness, love, success, and prosperity.

A treatment for Eternal Health: God-in-me is my eternal Source of health. From deep within the Source of God-in-me I receive an instant constant supply of health and strength, vim and vigor. God-in-me is my eternal health. Age does not lessen the health and strength that God is in me. Knowing God as my health heals me and keeps me well and heals others through me.

A treatment for Overflowing Happiness: God-in-me is my eternal Source of happiness. From deep within the Source of God-in-me I draw overflowing happiness. This happiness flows out from me every day in every way and I share it with others. The joy of the Lord is my strength. I make the world a happier place with my overflowing happiness.

A treatment for Overflowing Love: God-in-me is Love. The Love of God thinks and acts through me. I wish and think only good for myself, every one, and every thing. The Love of God pours itself out from me to everyone. I love because I am loved. As I permit the Love of God to operate in me this brings me together with all of the right people for every right purpose and keeps me in right relationships with everyone. My life is overflowing with Love in every right relationship. My whole experience of Life is a great romance.

A treatment for Overflowing Success and Prosperity: God-in-me is my overflowing source of success and prosperity. The mind, intelligence, and wisdom of God-in-me lead me into ways and means of success and prosperity. I cannot fail. I see and feel success. I see and feel NEW prosperity. I am always becoming greater and richer in God in every way. In God I am a success.

A treatment for Unlimited Money: The power of God-in-me is my power to get all of the good I desire. There is no limit to this "getting power" of God-in-me. By means of the getting power of God-in-me I get all of the good I desire. I see myself with an overflowing supply of money to use and enjoy. Thank you, God-in-me, for this overflowing supply of money and all good.

From My Prosperity Scrapbook

"The words 'I am' are potent words; be careful what you hitch them to. The thing you're claiming has a way of reaching back and claiming you."

— *A.L. Kitselman*

"God is a verb."

— *Buckminster Fuller*

In **Tuesdays With Morrie**, *Mitch Ablom's bestseller about a sportswriter who learns life's greatest lessons from his dying former college professor, Ablom asks Morrie why so many people are living unhappy lives. Morrie says, "Well, for one thing, the culture we have does not make people feel good about themselves. We're teaching the wrong things. And you have to be strong enough to say if the culture doesn't work, don't buy it. Create your own."*

- *If God had a refrigerator, your picture would be on it.*
- *If God had a wallet, your photo would be in it.*
- *God sends you flowers every spring and a sunrise every morning.*
- *When you want to talk, God will listen.*
- *God could live anywhere in the universe and yet chose your heart.*
- *And that Christmas gift God sent you in Bethlehem?*
- *Face it friend, God is crazy about you!*
- *... And remember: God answers Knee-Mail!*

— *Author Unknown*

God Says Yes To Me

I asked God if it was okay to be melodramatic and she said yes I asked her if it was okay to be short and she said it sure is and I asked her if I could wear nail polish or not wear nail polish and she said honey she calls me that sometimes she said you can do exactly what you want to Thanks God I said and is it even okay if I don't paragraph my letters Sweetcakes God said who knows where she picked that up what I'm telling you is Yes Yes Yes.

— *Steve Kowits*, In the Palm of Your Hand: The Poet's Portable Workshop

"Worrying is using your imagination to create something you don't want."

— *Unknown*

Something of God

I hear and behold God in every object, yet understand God not in the least,
Nor do I understand who there can be more wonderful than myself.
Why should I wish to see God better than this day?
I see something of God each hour of the twenty-four, and each moment then,
In the faces of men and women I see God, in my own face in the glass,
I find letters from God dropped in the street, and every one is signed by God's name,
And I leave them where they are, for I know that wheresoe'er I go
Others will punctually come forever and ever.

— Walt Whitman

A story about finding God...

There once was a little boy who wanted to meet God. He knew it was a long trip to where God lived, so he packed his suitcase with Twinkies and a six-pack of root beer, and he started his journey.

When he had gone about three blocks, he met an old woman. She was sitting in the park just staring at some pigeons. The boy sat down next to her and opened his suitcase. He was about to take a drink from his root beer when he noticed that the old lady looked hungry, so he offered her a Twinkie.

She gratefully accepted it and smiled at him. Her smile was so pretty that the boy wanted to see it again, so he offered her a root beer.

Once again, she smiled at him. They sat there all afternoon eating and smiling, but they never said a word.

As it grew dark, the boy realized how tired he was and he got up to leave but before he had gone more than a few steps he turned around, ran back to the old woman, and gave her a hug. She gave him her biggest smile ever.

When the boy opened the door to his own house a short time later his mother was surprised by the look of joy on his face. She asked him, "What did you do today that made you so happy?" He replied, "I had lunch with God and you know what? She's got the most beautiful smile I've ever seen!"

Meanwhile, the old woman, also radiant with joy, returned to her home. Her son was stunned by the look of peace on her face and he asked, "Mother, what did you do today that made you so happy?"

She replied, "I ate Twinkies in the park with God. You know, he's much younger than I expected."

— Author Unknown

The soft, gentle voice that calls you the Beloved has come to you in countless ways. Many people who have crossed your path have all sounded that voice in different tones. You have been cared for by many people with much tenderness and gentleness. You have been taught and instructed with much patience and perseverance. You have been encouraged to keep going when you were ready to give up and were stimulated to try again when you failed. You have been rewarded and praised for success ... but, somehow, all of these signs of love were not sufficient to convince you that you were the Beloved. Beneath all praises received remains the question: "If all those who showered me with so much attention could see me and know me in my innermost self, would they still love me?" That agonizing question, rooted in our innermost shadow, keeps persecuting us and makes us run away from the very place where that quiet voice calling us the Beloved can be heard.

We refuse to hear that voice that speaks from the very depths of us and says "You are my Beloved, on you my favor rests." That voice has always been there, but we are much more eager to listen to other, louder voices saying: "Prove that you are worth something; do something relevant, spectacular or powerful, and then you will learn the love you so desire." Meanwhile, the soft, gentle voice that speaks in the silence and solitude of our hearts remains unheard or, at least, unconvincing.

I invite you to listen to the voice of God with great inner attentiveness:
> I have called you by name from the very beginning.
> You are mine and I am yours.
> You are my beloved, on you my favor rests.
> I have molded you in the depths of the earth and knitted you together
> in your mother's womb.
> I have carved you in the palm of my hand and hidden you in the shadow
> of my embrace.
> I look at you with infinite tenderness and care for you with a care more
> intimate than that of a mother for her child.
> I have counted every hair on your head and guided you at every step.
> Wherever you go, I go with you, and wherever you rest, I keep watch.
> I will give you food that will satisfy all your hunger and drink that will
> quench all your thirst.
> I will not hide my face from you.
> You are my beloved in whom I am well pleased.

— *Adapted from Henri Nouwen's* The Beloved

The following very inspiring true story was shared by a woman who learned the power of changing her thoughts.

I would like to share my experience, strength, and hope. ...

About five years ago I cried for two days when I was told that I would have to become an athlete. I mean, there I was just a few tens of pounds away from 400. This was the equivalent of someone telling me to climb Mount Everest! I couldn't do it! It looked impossible, it felt impossible. It was impossible.

(My doctors) had told me that staying in bed (mostly) for almost ten years, had RUINED my metabolism. There was a period of time when consuming 800 calories per day would either make me gain weight or maintain perfectly.

I AM AN ATHLETE! I AM AN ATHLETE! This has been the mantra of my journey. ... The INCREDIBLE journey started with that INCREDULOUS thought: "I AM AN ATHLETE! I AM AN ATHLETE!" Then I walked out the door, and took the first step towards my mail box. Then months later, around the half block. Months more, around the full block. ... A year later, bopping to power-walking jock music, my weight was going down. Year 3, my neighbors' mouths were falling open, "Aren't you that girl who used to ride the bike with the flattened tires? What are you doing?" they would ask.

One man asked me, "What is the first thought that came to your mind when you started doing whatever it is that you have been doing with yourself?" And so I told him, "My first thought was that 'I am getting the hell out of this bed!' Beds are for sleeping, NOT LIVING! I was sick and tired of being sick and tired."

I AM AN ATHLETE! I AM AN ATHLETE! I am now power walking over sixteen miles per week, with interval jogging, mountain biking, and kickboxing. I am grateful that God allows me the constitution to keep on doing these things.

My journey started with a single step in the direction of the mail box at the end of my driveway.

NEVER GIVE UP! ! ! ! NEVER, EVER, EVER, EVER, — no, NEVER!

— *Jan K., Arlington, Texas*

"We have it in our power to begin the world again."

— Thomas Paine.

Continuing the above thought — We not only have the power to begin the world again — we use that power every moment of every day. However, most of us use our power the way we've always used it so the results are always the same. To get different results — we don't have to discover a new power, we must learn to use the power we already have differently.

— *Bert Carson, Daily Inspiration, November 6, 2000*
http://www.remember-thebook.com/dailyinspiration.htm

Enough

A time comes in your life when you finally get it ... When in the midst of all your fears and insanity you stop dead in your tracks and somewhere the voice inside your head cries out: ENOUGH! Enough fighting and crying or struggling to hold on. And, like a child quieting down after a blind tantrum, your sobs begin to subside, you shudder once or twice, you blink back your tears and through a mantle of wet lashes you begin to look at the world through new eyes. This is your awakening. You realize that it's time to stop hoping and waiting for something to change or for happiness, safety, and security to come galloping over the next horizon. You come to terms with the fact that he is not Prince Charming and you are not Cinderella and that in the real world there aren't always fairy tale endings (or beginnings for that matter) and that any guarantee of "happily ever after" must begin with you and in the process a sense of serenity is born of acceptance.

You awaken to the fact that you are not perfect and that not everyone will always love, appreciate, or approve of who or what you are...and that's OK. (They are entitled to their own views and opinions.) And you learn the importance of loving and championing yourself and in the process a sense of new found confidence is born of self-approval.

You stop judging and pointing fingers and you begin to accept people as they are and to overlook their shortcomings and human frailties and in the process a sense of peace and contentment is born of forgiveness. You realize that much of the way you view yourself, and the world around you is as a result of all the messages and opinions that have been ingrained into your psyche. And you begin to shift through all the crap you've been fed about how you should behave, how you should look and how much you should weigh, what you should wear, and where you should shop and what you should drive, and where you should live, and what you should do for a living, who you should sleep with, who you should marry and what you should expect of a marriage, the importance of having and raising children, or what you owe your parents.

And, you learn that alone does not mean lonely... And you look in the mirror and come to terms with the fact that you will never be a size 5 or a perfect 10 and you stop trying to compete with the image inside your head and agonizing over how you "stack up."

You also stop working so hard at putting your feelings aside, smoothing things over and ignoring your needs. You learn that feelings of entitlement are perfectly OK...and that it is your right to want things and to ask for the things that you want ... and that sometimes it is necessary to make demands.

You come to the realization that you deserve to be treated with love, kindness, sensitivity, and respect and you won't settle for less. And you allow only the hands of a lover who cherishes you to glorify you with his touch...and in the process you internalize the meaning of self-respect.

And you learn that your body really is your temple. And you begin to care for it and treat it with respect. You begin eating a balanced diet, drinking more water, and taking more time to exercise. You learn that fatigue diminishes the spirit and can create doubt and fear. So you take more time to rest. And, just as food fuels the body, laughter fuels the soul. So take more time to laugh and to play.

You learn that, for the most part, in life you get what you believe you deserve...and that much of life truly is a self fulfilling prophecy. You learn that anything worth achieving is worth working for and that wishing for something to happen is different from working toward making it happen. More importantly, you learn that in order to achieve success you need direction, discipline and perseverance. You also learn that no one can do it all alone and that it's OK to risk asking for help.

You learn that the only thing you must truly fear is the great robber baron of all time, FEAR itself. You learn to step right into and through your fears because you know that whatever happens you can handle it and to give in to fear is to give away the right to live life on your terms. And you learn to fight for your life and not to squander it living under a cloud of impending doom. You learn that life isn't always fair, you don't always get what you think you deserve and that sometimes bad things happen to unsuspecting, good people. On these occasions you learn not to personalize things. You learn that God isn't punishing you or failing to answer your prayers. It's just life happening.

And you learn to deal with evil in its most primal state — the ego. You learn that negative feelings such as anger, envy, and resentment must be understood and redirected or they will suffocate the life out of you and poison the universe that surrounds you. You learn to admit when you are wrong and to building bridges instead of walls.

Slowly, you begin to take responsibility for yourself by yourself and you make yourself a promise to never betray yourself and to never ever to settle for less than your heart's desire. And you hang a wind chime outside your window so you can listen to the wind. And you make it a point to keep smiling, to keep trusting, and to stay open to every wonderful possibility.

Finally, with courage in your heart and with God by your side you take a stand, you take a deep breath and you begin to design the life you want to live as best as you can.

— Author Unknown

What the Bible Says About It...

Do not be conformed to this world ... but be transformed (changed) by the (entire) renewal of your mind (by its new ideals and its new attitude). **Romans 12:2 AB**

For Jehovah God is our Light and our Protector. He gives grace and glory. No good thing will he withhold from those who walk along his paths. **Psalm 84:11 LB**

But now thus says the Lord, who created you. Be not afraid, for I have redeemed you; I have called you by your name; you are Mine. When you pass through the waters I will be with you, and when through the rivers, they shall not overwhelm you; when you go through fire you shall not be scorched; or through flames, you shall not be burned. For I am the Lord your God, the Holy One of Israel, your Savior. ... Because you are precious in My eyes, you are honored and I love you. ... Fear not, therefore, for I am with you. **Isaiah 43:1-5 MLB**

For the Lord thy God bringeth thee into a good land, a land of brooks of water, of fountains and depths that spring out of valleys and hills; A land of wheat, and barley and vines, and fig trees; and pomegranates; a land of oil olive, and honey; A land wherein thou shalt eat bread without scarceness, thou shalt not lack any thing in it; a land whose stones are iron, and out of whose hills thou mayest dig brass. When thou hast eaten and art full, then thou shalt bless the Lord thy God for the good land which he hath given thee. **Deuteronomy 8:7-10 KJV**

Delight yourself also in the Lord, and He will give you the desires and secret petitions of your heart. Commit your way to the Lord (roll and repose each care of your load on Him); trust (lean on, rely on, and be confident) also in Him and He will bring it to pass. **Psalm 37:4,5 AB**

You are my hiding place from every storm of life; you even keep me from getting into trouble! You surround me with songs of victory! I will instruct you (says the Lord) and guide you along the best pathway for your life; I will advise you and watch your progress. **Psalm 32:7,8 LB**

Because the Lord is my Shepherd, I have everything I need. He lets me rest in the meadow grass and leads me beside the quiet streams. He restores my failing health. He helps me do what honors him the most. Even when walking through the dark valley of death I will not be afraid, for you are close beside me, guarding, guiding all the way. You provide delicious food for me in the presence of my enemies. You have welcomed me as your guest; blessings overflow! Your goodness and unfailing kindness shall be with me all of my life, and afterwards I will live with you forever in your home. **Psalm 23:1-6 LB**

...they that seek the Lord shall not want any good thing. **Psalm 34:10 KJV**

I love all who love me. Those who search for me shall surely find me. Unending riches, honor, justice and righteousness are mine to distribute. My gifts are better than the purest gold or sterling silver! My paths are those of justice and right. Those who love and follow me are indeed wealthy. I fill their treasuries. **Proverbs 8:17-21 LB**

I have loved you, O my people, with an everlasting love; with lovingkindness I have drawn you to me. **Jeremiah 31:3 LB**

Therefore I tell you, do not be anxious about your life, what you shall eat or what you shall drink, nor about your body, what you shall put on. Is not life more than food, and the body more than clothing? Look at the birds of the air: they neither sow nor reap nor gather into barns, and yet your heavenly Father feeds them. Are you not of more value than they? And which of you by being anxious can add one bit to his span of life? And why are you anxious about clothing? Consider the lilies of the field, how they grow; they neither toil nor spin; yet I tell you, even Solomon in all his glory was not arrayed like one of these. But if God so clothes the grass of the field, which today is alive and tomorrow is thrown into the oven, will he not much more clothe you, O men of little faith? Therefore do not be anxious, saying, "What shall we eat?" or "What shall we drink?" or "What shall we wear?" For the Gentiles seek all these things; and your heavenly Father knows that you need them all. But seek first his kingdom and his righteousness, and all these things shall be yours as well. **Matthew 6:25-34 RSV**

Fear not, little flock, for your Father is pleased to give you the kingdom. **Luke 12:32 MLB**

Are not five sparrows sold for two pennies? And not one of them is forgotten before God. Why, even the hairs of your head are all numbered. Fear not; you are of more value than many sparrows. **Luke 12: 6,7 RSV**

The God who made the world and all it contains, who is Lord of heaven and earth, does not dwell in temples built by human hands, neither is He served by human hands as if He lacked anything — He, the Giver of life and breath and all things to every one. He has made from one person every nation of men...so that they might seek for God, if only they would feel for and find Him, although He is not far from each of us; for "in Him we live and move and have our being." And some of your own poets have expressed themselves, "for we are also His offspring." **Acts 17: 24-28 MLB**

May your roots go down deep into the soil of God's marvelous love; and may you be able to feel and understand, as all God's children should, how long, how wide, how deep, and how high his love really is; and to experience this love for yourselves, though it is so great that you will never see the end of it or fully know or understand it. Now glory be to God who by his mighty power at work within us is able to do far more than we would ever dare to ask or even dream of — infinitely beyond our highest prayers, desires, thoughts, or hopes. **Ephesians 3:17-20 LB**

And my God will fully supply all your needs according to His abundant wealth so glorious in Christ Jesus. **Philippians 4:19 MLB**

For whoever would draw near to God must believe that he exists and that he rewards those who seek him. **Hebrews 11:6 RSV**

So we know and believe the love God has for us. God is love, and he who abides in love abides in God, and God abides in him. **I John 4:16 RSV**

For I am persuaded beyond doubt (am sure) that neither death nor life, nor angels nor principalities, nor things impending and threatening nor things to come, nor powers, Nor height nor depth, nor anything else in all creation will be able to separate us from the love of God. **Romans 8:38,29 AB**

Let him have all your worries and cares, for he is always thinking about you and watching everything that concerns you. **I Peter 5:7 LB**

And He will establish you to the end (keep you steadfast, give you strength, and guarantee your vindication: He will be your warrant against all accusation or indictment so that you will be) guiltless and irreproachable in the day of our Lord Jesus Christ (the Messiah). God is faithful (reliable, trustworthy, and therefore ever true to His promise, and He can be depended on); by Him you were called into companionship and participation with His Son, Jesus Christ our Lord. **I Corinthians 1:8,9 AB**

Abbreviations:

AB = Amplified Bible
KJV = King James Version
LB = Living Bible
MLB = Modern Living Bible
RSV = Revised Standard Version

Chapter 2: The Power of Gratitude

"If the only prayer you say in your whole life is 'thank you,'
that would suffice."
—Meister Eckhart

Let's review for a moment our definition of prosperity: Prosperity is the continuous process of joyfully receiving an abundance of everything that we need, and joyfully giving back from the overflow.

Can you see how it would be impossible to experience prosperity without gratitude? How can we joyfully receive if we are not grateful? And why in the world would we joyfully give back if we were not grateful?

If you want more to be grateful for, try being more grateful for what you already have.

Cultivating an attitude of gratitude will increase the flow of good into your life. Every one of us has innumerable blessings in our life to be grateful for. Consciously acknowledging the good increases the good. Gratitude saves us from toxic self-pity, which is the polar opposite of prosperity consciousness.

When I was very new in twelve-step recovery I went to a meeting one night and when the meeting was opened up for sharing, I talked about how depressed I was. I went on and on about it. The other people at the meeting kindly and patiently listened. Finally, I passed and the next person shared.

After the meeting an old-timer in the program came up to me with a smile on her face and said, "You know what depression is, don't you?" Now understand — by this time I was a licensed mental health professional; I thought I understood depression very well. But her question caught me off-guard, and I said something like, "Huh?"

She nailed me: "Depression is terminal self-pity. The cure is gratitude." With another smile, she walked away.

I left the meeting steaming! How dare she?!

As I drove home, I began to realize she was absolutely right! I did have a lot of self-pity that was keeping me depressed! I decided that if she was right about that much, she might also be right about "the cure is gratitude." So I made a decision to start consciously practicing an attitude of gratitude. The results were immediate and dramatic! Practicing gratitude helped free me from a life-long struggle with self-pity and depression.

I will never forget a young woman who shared her gratitude at a meeting of Narcotics

Anonymous. She said, "I am so grateful that I have had a shower today. Not long ago, I was living on the street and I had no way to take a shower. Now I usually take two showers a day and I am so grateful for my warm showers." I think of this young woman every day when I take my warm shower and I am very grateful.

My mother was a great teacher of gratitude. No matter what difficulty or disappointment she might be facing, she always looked for blessings to be grateful for, and she always found them! She had a small decorative plaque in her kitchen that read:

"Thank God for dirty dishes, — They have a tale to tell.
While other folks go hungry — We're eating very well.
With home, health, and happiness — We shouldn't want to fuss.
For by this stack of evidence, — God's very good to us."

Can you look at a stack of dirty dishes and give thanks? Are you willing to learn?

Start by being grateful for being alive. Your life force is greater than your death force, or you would not be alive.

Be grateful for your body, all of its intricate miraculous systems, and all of your senses.

Pause for a moment before each meal, and be grateful for your food and for all that nourishes and sustains you.

Be grateful for every teacher (even your ex-husband or ex-wife!) and for every learning experience you have ever attracted/created.

Be grateful for the beauty of nature, for art, for music, for books and the ability to read.

If you live in the United States, be grateful that you live in the most prosperous, the most democratic society ever known on Earth.

Unless you are dying of starvation and exposure — drawing your last breath — you have some means of support. If you have any income or source of support, be grateful! Being grateful for what you are now receiving will open the channels for you to receive more.

If you have debts and bills to pay, be grateful to every one of your creditors! The Universe has trusted you and has loaned you goods and services for your convenience. Be grateful for every check you write — every bill you pay.

Openly acknowledge your gratitude to the people who have made a positive difference in your life. Let them know you appreciate them. Put it in writing. Get in the habit of writing thank you notes.

Don't forget to appreciate your Self! Appreciate your strength — it's there or you would never have survived to this point! Appreciate your own beauty. (Every one is uniquely beautiful. The more you acknowledge and appreciate your own beauty, the more you will appreciate the beauty of others.) Appreciate your creativity. Appreciate your generosity and your ability to love. Appreciate your perseverance — you have never completely given up, even though you may have been tempted many times. (If you had, you would not be here reading this book.) Appreciate your sense of humor — it's there or you would never have survived to this point! **Appreciate your divinity. You are a spiritual being on a human journey.**

Exercises

♥   Journal writing assignment: For 30 days, write down at least five things a day that you are grateful for. Be very specific. Once you have written one thing down on your gratitude list, do not repeat it. Be consciously aware as you go through your day of new things to add to your gratitude list.

When you have done this for 30 days, you will have developed a habit of looking for blessings and finding them.

This 30-day assignment started on: ___/___/___ (date) and completed on ___/___/___ (date).

♥   To Do: Write at least one thank you note or gratitude letter to one living person who has made a significant positive difference in your life. Mail or deliver the letter to them.

This letter or note written to _____ and mailed/delivered on: ___/___/___ (date).

♥   Discuss this journal/letter-writing process with your prosperity partner(s).

Discussed on: ___/___/___ (date)

Affirmations

I am truly thankful for all the good I already receive.

Every day I take time to count my blessings.

I am grateful each day for life's unlimited possibilities.

I am grateful for my friends and prosperity partners.

I am grateful for musicians, painters, authors, and poets.

I am grateful that good is available to me now.

I am grateful for all of the gifts I have been given.

I am grateful I am guided into Truth.

I am grateful for every teacher of Truth I have known.

I am grateful to be alive, happy, and healthy. I love life and life is GOOD!

From My Prosperity Scrapbook

I Am Thankful For...

...the mess to clean after a party because it means I have been surrounded by friends.

...the taxes I pay because it means that I'm employed.

...the clothes that fit a little too snug because it means I have enough to eat.

...a lawn that needs mowing, windows that need cleaning, and gutters that need fixing because it means I have a home.

...all the complaining I hear about our government because it means we have freedom of speech.

...the spot at the far end of the parking lot because it means I am capable of walking.

...my huge heating bill because it means I am warm.

...the lady behind me in church who sings off-key because it means I can hear.

...the piles of laundry and ironing because it means my loved ones are nearby.

...weariness and aching muscles at the end of the day because it means I have been productive.

...the alarm that goes off in the early morning hours because it means I'm alive.

— *Author Unknown*

This Being Human

This being human is a guest house.
Every Morning a new arrival.

A joy, a depression, a meanness,
Some momentary awareness comes
as an unexpected visitor.

Welcome and entertain them all!
Even if they're a crowd of sorrows,
who violently sweep your house
empty of its furniture,
still, treat each guest honorably.
He may be clearing you out
for some new delight.

The dark thought, the shame, the malice,
meet them at the door laughing,
and invite them in.

Be grateful for whoever comes,
Because each has been sent
as a guide from beyond.

— Rumi,
thirteenth century Sufi mystic

"An exercise I try to practice is to try for a full inventory of my blessings and then for a right acceptance of the many gifts that are mine — both temporal and spiritual. Here I try to achieve a state of joyful gratitude. When such a brand of gratitude is repeatedly affirmed and pondered, it can finally displace the natural tendency to congratulate myself on whatever progress I may have been able to make in some areas of living. I try to hold fast to the truth that a full and thankful heart cannot entertain great conceits. When brimming with gratitude, one's heartbeat must surely result in outgoing love, the finest emotion that we can ever know."

— Bill W., 1988 AA Grapevine, Inc,
"The Language of the Heart," p. 271

What the Bible Says About It...

Make a joyful noise to the Lord, all you lands!...Enter into His gates with thanksgiving and a thank offering and into His courts with praise! Be thankful and say so to Him, bless and affectionately praise His name. **Psalms 100: 1, 4 AB**

Speak out to one another in psalms and hymns and spiritual songs, offering praise with voices (and instruments) and making melody with all your heart to the Lord. At all times and for everything giving thanks in the name of our Lord Jesus Christ to God the Father. **Ephesians 5:19-20 AB**

Don't worry about anything; instead, pray about everything; tell God your needs and don't forget to thank him for his answers. **Philippians 4:6 MLB**

Do not fret or have any anxiety about anything, but in every circumstance and in everything, by prayer and petition (definite requests), with thanksgiving, continue to make your wants known to God. **Philippians 4:6 AB**

Let the peace of heart which comes from Christ be always present in your hearts and lives, for this is your responsibility and privilege as members of his body. And always be thankful. **Colossians 3:15 LB**

Rejoice evermore. Pray without ceasing. In every thing give thanks: for this is the will of God in Christ Jesus concerning you. **I Thessalonians 5:16-18 KJV**

Abbreviations:
AB = Amplified Bible
KJV = King James Version
LB = Living Bible
MLB = Modern Living Bible
RSV = Revised Standard Version

Chapter 3: The Power of the Law of Circulation

"Give generously, for your gifts will return to you later."
-The Hebrew Bible, Ecclesiastes 11:1 (Living Bible Translation)

Simply stated, the law of circulation says that whatever you give or send out into the Universe will return to you multiplied.

Every major faith tradition on planet Earth teaches the law of circulation. Jesus of Nazareth, the carpenter rabbi said, "You will reap what you sow." Eastern religions teach the law of circulation as karma. Twelve-step fellowships teach this profound spiritual paradox: "The way to keep what you have is by giving it away."

In common English we say, "What goes around, comes around." Quantum physics calls it the law of cause and effect. In agriculture, we return the best seed to the ground in order to receive next season's harvest.

Whatever you call it, the important thing is to be consciously aware of the law of circulation and consciously use it to attract and create what you want in your life.

Typically, people send out a mixture of positive and negative energy and receive back a mixture of positive and negative energy. Also typically, they see no relationship between what they send out and what they get back! They overlook the positive, focus on the negative, and see themselves as helpless victims at the mercy of fate.

As a spiritually mature, conscious person, you can choose what you send out and therefore determine what you receive in return! You already have begun this process in chapters one and two, with understanding the power of your thoughts and the power of gratitude. Consciously choosing positive thoughts simultaneously sends positive energy out into the Universe and sends positive energy in — into your heart, into your soul, and into your mind. Gratitude is a very focused form of positive thought that always draws positive energy back to it.

Jesus also said, "Freely you have received. Freely give." **The law of circulation will work powerfully in your favor when you joyfully acknowledge all of the good you have already received and give back out of your gratitude.**

Every one of us has received some measure of good into our lives or we would never have survived our infancies and childhoods. As children, someone cared for us at least enough to keep us alive. We are now adults receiving some form of support from

> In common English we say, "What goes around, comes around."

the Universe or we could not survive as adults. To keep this flow of good coming into our lives and to increase the flow, part of our spiritual work is to gratefully and joyfully acknowledge this good by giving back or circulating the good.

So, for example, if we want more love in our lives, we gratefully and joyfully acknowledge and affirm the love we already have received and we open our hearts and give love to others. We thus become a channel, or conduit, of universal, divine, infinite Love and the more we give — unconditionally, without attachment, out of gratitude — the more we receive.

(I make the point that love must be given unconditionally, without attachment, out of gratitude for love already received, because much of what is called "love" in our culture is NOT love because it is given with conditions, with expectations of reciprocity, and with strings attached. The unspoken agreement is something like, "I will love you under the following conditions and if you meet all of my expectations and with the understanding that you will love me equally in return and express that love in precisely the way I want you to express it." In fact, much of what we call love and romance in our culture is a combination of codependency and sexual attraction — but that's another workbook! For now, just remember — love is by definition unconditional — given with no strings attached.)

Using the law of circulation, if we want more money in our lives we gratefully and joyfully acknowledge what we already have received and we gratefully and joyfully give money back — to people, places, and institutions where we receive our spiritual food and to those in need, as our inner guidance directs. When we give this money we give it without condition or attachment. This specific application of the law of circulation is also taught by every major faith tradition on planet Earth and is called *tithing*.

Unfortunately, in dominant Western culture the word tithing has come to be associated with shame-based, fundamentalist religions that teach tithing as an obligation to be met out of fear. ("If you don't do this, God will get you!") I invite you along with me to reclaim this joyful practice for your spiritual growth and prosperity.

The word tithe literally means a "tenth" and the standard teaching is to give away one tenth of your income in order to maintain spiritual integrity. This idea will shock and terrify some people! Here is my personal experience.

When I first received this teaching in the late 1980s I was working in a high-stress middle management position, making about $30,000 per year. I began immediately to give 10 percent of my income to people, places, and institutions where I received spiritual food. At the time, I was not active in a church so I did not give to any church. However, I was receiving spiritual food from a variety of sources — twelve-step groups, individuals, books, tapes, etc. — so I regularly gave money to these sources.

In pursuing my true purpose, I soon decided to quit my job and start my private therapy practice — a dream I had held for many years. At the time I had no savings, no financial cushion of any kind. I had a mortgage, car and credit card payments to make, as well as my own living expenses. As with any new business or practice, in the beginning money (income) came to me in little dribbles. With every little bit that came in I said, "Thank you, Godde!" I kept exact records of my income and

I continued to tithe 10 percent of my gross income to the penny — 10 percent before expenses were deducted and taxes were paid.

Was I afraid? Of course I was afraid! But *I acted as if I was not afraid.* I kept listening to my prosperity tapes and kept affirming my positive thoughts (for example, "the Universe always supports me" and "Godde is supplying all of my needs today"). I stayed focused on what I wanted — and one of the things I wanted was to pay all of my bills on time. So I kept reminding the Universe that I wanted to pay all of my bills on time. And I kept affirming that I serve Godde and money serves me. And I kept tithing. *All of my bills got paid on time with money I had left over after I tithed.*

> *Of course I was afraid! But I acted as if I was not afraid.*

Just a few months after I started my practice a major international corporation contacted me. They were looking for a mental health professional to provide services to their employees in my area. After some brief, informal discussions — with virtually no effort on my part — they awarded me a contract to provide these services. The contract was written in such a way that I was available to their hundreds of employees and to their employees' family members and the company paid me for being available whether the employees used my services or not.

The bottom line: For five years afterward, I received a large check in the mail every month for providing quality mental health services, whenever requested, to the employees and family members of this large corporation. For most of that time, the work involved in fulfilling this contract required a relatively small amount of my time. The income from the contract provided a steady source of money — more than enough to meet my overhead and living expenses. I was free to develop my practice in certain areas of specialization — just as I had always dreamed of doing. Having the steady income from that contract, I also was able to negotiate lower fees with some clients who were financially challenged — always affirming their prosperity, their worthiness, and their ability to pay.

I remembered that the income from the contract, or from other clients, was not my source of supply. My ultimate true source of supply was a generous, loving Universe that brought back to me multiplied the good I was giving.

After a few years I had a six-figure income, more money than I could have imagined earning at one time in my life. I continued to tithe, but became less attentive to giving exactly 10 percent to the penny. I am not a numbers person; numbers and exact percentages and decimal points do not excite me. In fact, they tend to frustrate and bore me. By this time, I knew that *everything I am and everything I have belongs to Godde.* So I continued to tithe regularly and generously to people, places, and institutions where I received spiritual food and to people in need. I gave my tithes in joy and gratitude, without conditions or attachment.

There is some disagreement among spiritual leaders as to the appropriateness of giving tithes to people in need. My reading of Scripture indicates to me that giving to people in need is appropriate and blessed by Godde. (For example, read the story of Cornelius in the book of Acts starting at chapter ten.) I am conscious, however, of giving in a way that encourages self-responsibility instead of dependency. For example, my husband and I make a monthly contribution to Habitat for Humanity. This organization assists low-income families in a way that empowers the family and preserves their dignity.

I would encourage anyone who chooses to honor the law of circulation by tithing to go inside and ask your inner wisdom where to give your tithes. Some readers may say, "I don't know where to give because I am not receiving any spiritual food." To those readers I would say, that is the first thing you want to change! **Get your soul fed on a regular basis!**

Get your soul fed on a regular basis!

Go somewhere and do something that will strengthen you, build your self-esteem, remind you of the Truth, honor the highest and best within you and within all of creation. The Universe has many channels through which you can receive "soul food." There may or may not be a church or formal religious fellowship in your area that is a good fit for you right now. If not, your soul can be fed by music, art, spiritual literature, nature, individuals, informal groups or fellowships. Start consciously seeking to have your soul fed on a regular basis and as you begin to receive spiritual food, start giving back in order to stay in the flow.

I have given tithe checks to friends, to twelve-step groups, to churches, to museums, to authors of books, and to conference speakers. For example, a number of years ago I attended a women's conference. The keynote speaker, Hedy Schleifer, really inspired me with her warmth, her courage, and her zest for life. After her talk I made it a point to meet her and to get her business card. After the conference I sent her a check for $200 along with a note, explaining that part of my spiritual program is to give a portion of my income to people from whom I receive spiritual food. I told her that her speech at the conference had fed my soul and I felt that it was appropriate to share some of my tithes for that month with her. She graciously acknowledged my gift and told me that she had decided to divide the check and donate $100 to two of her favorite community organizations. By the way, this started an ongoing correspondence with this beautiful lady that fed my soul for several years!

Here are some of the benefits of tithing I have experienced or, the top eleven reasons why I tithe:

1) Tithing tangibly demonstrates my gratitude for what I already have received.
2) Tithing tangibly demonstrates my faith that the Universe will continue to supply everything I need.
3) Tithing tangibly demonstrates my belief that we are all connected.
4) Tithing tangibly demonstrates that "I serve the Universe. Money serves me."
5) Tithing tangibly demonstrates my willingness to honor the universal laws of prosperity.
6) Tithing keeps me in the flow of inexhaustible supply.
7) Tithing neutralizes my fears about money.

8) Tithing makes me more consciously aware of where I am receiving my spiritual food.

9) Tithing regularly and systematically establishes order, harmony, and a gentle discipline in my financial affairs.

10) Tithing reminds me that everything I am and everything I have belongs to Godde.

11) Tithing is fun! It makes me feel rich!

Please take note: When I say tithing demonstrates something, what I mean is that tithing demonstrates that thing TO ME. I do not need to prove or demonstrate to anyone or anything *out there* my gratitude, my faith, or my belief that we are all connected. I demonstrate and affirm these things *to myself* tangibly every time I write a tithe check and give it away.

I emphasize the word tangibly. There is a part of my human mind that needs tangible demonstrations or visual aids. It takes one level of faith to *say,* "I am grateful for all of the gifts I have received and I know the Universe will continue to supply my needs, and I know that I am connected with all of life, etc., etc." It takes another level of faith to pull out my checkbook, write the check, sign it, and mail it or give it away. This is a tangible demonstration of my beliefs.

Tithing is an extremely powerful and effective affirmation that builds my faith continuously. **Tithing is one of the most joyful things I do.**

When I attracted my ideal spiritual partner and we got married and combined our financial matters, we discussed at length our values and beliefs about money. In an attitude of mutual love and respect we have created a system of giving, saving, investing, and using money that is comfortable for both of us. The Universe continues to bless us abundantly.

Now in our late forties, we have the financial resources so that if we never earn another penny we could continue living at our present very comfortable standard of living to the age of 100 and still leave a significant inheritance to our heirs. In fact, we could live much more extravagantly, never earn another penny, live to be 100, and still leave a significant estate. We choose to live relatively simply because it suits us. (We did, however, recently buy a brand new $95,000 tow truck to pull our RV!)

Does this kind of financial independence sound like an impossible dream to you? Don't you believe it for a minute! Again, as I told you in the Introduction to this workbook, the Universe does not play favorites. Both my husband and I came from working class families. Neither of us have inherited financial assets. We have created and attracted our good by honoring and using the principles described in this workbook.

Are you willing to honor the principle of tithing in order to increase the flow of good into your life? Again, you do not have to believe the law will work — only *act as if* you believe it.

Here's what to do: If you are willing to give 10 percent of your income to people, places, and institutions where you receive spiritual food and to people in need, GREAT! If you are not yet willing, choose a percentage between 1 percent and 10 percent. Follow these instructions for at least the next three months, using whatever percentage you have chosen. At the end of three months, increase your giving by at least 1 percent. Continue increasing your giving quarterly by at least 1 percent until you are giving at least 10 percent.

Exercises

♥ **Complete this statement:** Beginning immediately, I will give at least _____ percent of my income to people, places, and institutions where I receive my spiritual food and to people in need. I will give in gratitude without condition or attachment. I will seek the guidance of my inner wisdom in determining where I give my tithes. (If this percentage is less that 10 percent, I will increase my giving by at least 1 percent every three months until I am giving at least 10 percent.)

_____   ___/___/___

(signature)   (date)

Shared with prosperity partner(s) on: ___/___/___ (date).

♥ **Journal writing assignment:** In your journal, start a new section tabbed "Tithing Journal." With each page in this section of your journal, draw a line down the center of the page to create two columns. On the left side of the page write "income" at the top of the column. On the right side of the page write "tithe given" at the top of the column.

Beginning with the very next income you receive, write the amount of the income in the left column and the date you received it. Record all income from any source. In the right-hand column, beside the amount of income you have recorded, keep a record of what tithes you give — the amount you give and to whom and the date you give it. Continue to record your income and your tithing.

I strongly suggest that you write your tithe checks first, then write the rest of your checks. This is the best way I have found to maintain spiritual integrity. As you write ALL of your checks, affirm your gratitude and your belief that the Universe will continue to supply all of your needs.

Some of my readers may be thinking, "So you say that this stuff is guaranteed. If I try tithing and it doesn't work for me, are you going to refund all the money I've given away?" Now think for a minute. What kind of energy would you be sending out into the Universe with this kind of attitude — looking for a "loophole"? The answer is "no." If for some reason you are not satisfied with the results of your tithing, I will not refund your money to you. By promising to do so I would be sabotaging, undermining, and circumventing your prosperity. If you are going to successfully use the law of circulation, you must have faith in a power much greater than Grace Terry. Or you must at least act as if you do!

Keep breathing, keep affirming the positive, and keep imagining the highest and best manifesting in your life. **Practice extravagant generosity in all areas of your life. Be lavishly generous with your time, your talents, your energy, your emotional support, your love, AND your money.** Give without reservation and without attachment. Know that all you give in gratitude will return to you multiplied. *Also be conscious to do whatever you need to do to regularly receive an infusion of energy, love, and emotional support.*

Practice receiving AND giving.

Affirmations

I serve the Universe. Money serves me.

I love to give and the Universe loves to give to me.

I am a great receiver because I am a great giver.

Because I serve the Universe, I have a right to an abundant life.

I love to tithe where I receive my spiritual food.

I give lavishly and joyously and receive abundantly and thankfully.

As I give, I receive. I give my best and I expect the best of everything in return.

Because I give freely and generously of my time, energy, love, and money, I am in the flow of inexhaustible supply.

I am a millionaire because I give a million dollars' worth of service to the world.

I am in the business of giving, loving, and serving.

I prosper everyone and everyone prospers me.

My giving is making me rich.*

Voluntary, faithful tithing of my whole income now activates the law of ever-increasing prosperity for me. I now tithe my way to prosperity.*

(*from the writings of Catherine Ponder, Palm Desert, California, 1971)

From My Prosperity Scrapbook

The following is a great story about how one little girl created abundance for herself and for others.

Wait! I Have a Plan

by Janet Detter Margul, Plano, Texas, USA

When my daughter Lisa was in kindergarten, for her sixth birthday she asked if she could invite not only her whole class to her party, but the other class at school too. I probably turned pale at the thought of 60 kindergartners at a party because she said quickly, "Wait! Don't say no yet. I have a plan."

I was already thinking about how she'd been making a birthday wish list for weeks — that's one way to get a lot of presents! But I let her tell me her plan. She wanted to invite a lot of people to a picnic in the park, and ask them if, instead of bringing gifts, they could bring food to give the food pantry.

Just the month before, her scout troop took a field trip to the local food pantry, taking canned goods we'd collected for a service project. Lisa explained that the lady there said it looked like they had a lot of food, but come spring all that food would be gone and many people would be hungry. She thought that if she asked for food for her party, the people wouldn't be so hungry in May.

Well, I had to say yes to that, but I was worried she'd regret giving up all her birthday presents for food. I kept asking if she was sure she wanted to do this. Finally she explained, "Mom, you know I always get a bunch of junkie presents at birthday parties. I'd rather have food to give instead of those. Besides, the people who give good presents, well, you know they'll give me food AND good presents anyway."

So we had the party in the park, with a cotton candy machine, hot dogs, and jugs and jugs of lemonade. A ton of kids came, and some adults. Lisa was just beside herself when someone gave her TWO cans of food. Some gave big bags of food. It was like a one-child food drive. I was overwhelmed at how much food. We filled up two station wagons with it.

There was too much to take home and then take to the food pantry later, so we went straight there from the park. We arrived pretty late in the day, close to closing time. My tiny kindergartner marched into the building and told the volunteer at the desk, "I've got some food to give you."

The volunteer smiled down at her and said, "Well, bring it on in, honey." Lisa said, "But it's a LOT of food," so the volunteer got a shopping cart to help Lisa bring in her donation. The volunteer was obviously thinking of a "child's size" donation but, once she saw all the food, she just boggled.

Lisa handed her one of her party invitations "So's you know how I got so much," and the volunteer started to cry. I, and the other adults, joined her. Lisa looked up at us and announced, "Stop crying. I'll help carry it in."

Receiving by Giving

James Bender, in his book How to Talk Well *(New York: McGraw-Hill Book Company, Inc., 1994) relates the story of a farmer who grew award-winning corn. Each year he entered his corn in the state fair where it won a blue ribbon. One year a newspaper reporter interviewed him and learned something interesting about how he grew it.*

The reporter discovered that the farmer shared his seed corn with his neighbors. "How can you afford to share your best seed corn with your neighbors when they are entering corn in competition with yours each year?" the reporter asked.

"Why, sir," said the farmer, "didn't you know? The wind picks up pollen from the ripening corn and swirls it from field to field. If my neighbors grow inferior corn, cross-pollination will steadily degrade the quality of my corn. If I am to grow good corn, I must help my neighbors grow good corn."

He is very much aware of the connectedness of life. His corn cannot improve unless his neighbor's corn also improves.

Various versions of the following story were circulated through the Human Potential Movement of the 1960s and '70s. The following version was included in the book Scripts People Live, *by Claude Steiner. I see it as a powerful metaphor for the law of circulation.*

A Fuzzy Tale

Once upon a time, a long time ago, there lived two very happy people called Tim and Maggie with two children called John and Lucy. To understand how happy they were, you have to understand how things were in those days. You see, in those days everyone was given at birth a small, soft, Fuzzy Bag. Anytime a person reached into this bag he was able to pull out a Warm Fuzzy. Warm Fuzzies were very much in demand because whenever somebody was given a Warm Fuzzy it made him feel warm and fuzzy all over. People who didn't get Warm Fuzzies regularly were in danger of developing a sickness in their back which caused them to shrivel up and die.

In those days it was very easy to get Warm Fuzzies. Anytime that somebody felt like it, he might walk up to you and say, "I'd like to have a Warm Fuzzy." You would then reach into your bag and pull out a Fuzzy the size of a little girl's hand. As soon as the Fuzzy saw the light of day it would smile and blossom into a large, shaggy, Warm Fuzzy. You then would lay it on the person's shoulder or head or lap and it would snuggle up and melt right against their skin and make them feel good all over. People were always asking each other for Warm Fuzzies, and since they were always given freely, getting enough of them was never a problem. There were always plenty to go around, and as a consequence everyone was happy and felt warm and fuzzy most of the time.

One day a bad witch became angry because everyone was so happy and no one was buying potions and salves. The witch was very clever and devised a very wicked plan. One beautiful morning the witch crept up to Tim while Maggie was playing with their daughter and whispered in his ear, "See here, Tim, look at all the Fuzzies that Maggie is giving to Lucy. You know, if she keeps it up, eventually she is going to run out and then there won't be any left for you!"

Tim was astonished. He turned to the witch and said, "Do you mean to tell me that there isn't a Warm Fuzzy in our bag every time we reach into it?"

And the witch said, "No, absolutely not, and once you run out, that's it. You don't have any more." With this the witch flew away on a broom, laughing and cackling all the way.

Tim took this to heart and began to notice every time Maggie gave up a Warm Fuzzy to somebody else. Eventually he got very worried and upset because he liked Maggie's Warm Fuzzies very much and did not want to give them up. He certainly did not think it was right for Maggie to be spending all her Warm Fuzzies on the children and on other people. He began to complain every time he saw Maggie giving a Warm Fuzzy to somebody else, and because Maggie liked him very much, she stopped giving Warm Fuzzies to other people as often, and reserved them for him.

The children watched this and soon began to get the idea that it was wrong to give up Warm Fuzzies any time you were asked or felt like it. They too became very careful. They would watch their parents closely and whenever they felt that one of their parents was giving away too many Fuzzies to others, they also began to object. They began to feel worried whenever they gave away too many Warm Fuzzies. Even though they found a Warm Fuzzy every time they reached into their bag, they reached in less and less and became more and more stingy. Soon people began to notice the lack of Warm Fuzzies, and they began to feel less warm and less fuzzy. They began to shrivel up and occasionally, people would die from lack of Warm Fuzzies. More and more people went to the witch to buy potions and salves even though they didn't seem to work.

Well, the situation was getting very serious indeed. The bad witch who had been watching all of this didn't really want the people to die (since dead people couldn't buy his salves and potions), so a new plan was devised. Everyone was given a bag that was very similar to the Fuzzy Bag except that this one was cold while the Fuzzy Bag was warm. Inside of the witch's bag were Cold Pricklies. These cold pricklies did not make people feel warm and fuzzy, but made them feel cold and prickly instead. But, they did prevent people's backs from shriveling up. So, from then on, every time somebody said, "I want a Warm Fuzzy," people who were worried about depleting their supply would say, "I can't give you a Warm Fuzzy, but would you like a Cold Prickly?" Sometimes, two people would walk up to each other, thinking they could get a Warm Fuzzy, but one or the other of them would change his mind and they would wind up giving each other Cold Pricklies. So, the end result was that while very few people were dying, a lot of people were sad, unhappy, and feeling very cold and prickly.

The situation got very complicated because, since the coming of the witch, there were less and less Warm Fuzzies around; so Warm Fuzzies, which used to be thought of as free as air, became extremely valuable. This caused people to do all sorts of things in order to obtain them. Before the witch had appeared, people used to gather in groups of three, four, or five, never caring too much who was giving Warm Fuzzies to whom. After the coming of the witch, people began to pair off and to reserve all their Warm Fuzzies for each other exclusively. People who forgot themselves and gave a Warm Fuzzy to someone else would immediately feel guilty about it because they knew that their partner would probably resent the loss of a Warm Fuzzy. People who could not find a generous partner had to buy their Warm Fuzzies and had to work long hours to earn the money.

Some people somehow became "popular" and got a lot of Warm Fuzzies without having to return them. These people would then sell these Warm Fuzzies to people who were "unpopular" and needed them to survive.

Another thing which happened was that some people would take Cold Pricklies — which were limitless and freely available — coat them white and fluffy and pass them on as Warm Fuzzies. These counterfeit Warm Fuzzies were really Plastic Fuzzies, and they caused additional difficulties. For instance, two people would get together and freely exchange Plastic Fuzzies, which presumably should have made them feel good, but they came away feeling bad instead. Since they thought they had been exchanging Warm Fuzzies, people grew very confused about this, never realizing that their cold prickly feelings were really the result of the fact they had been given a lot of Plastic Fuzzies.

So the situation was very, very dismal and it all started because of the witch who made people believe that some day, when least expected, they might reach into their Warm Fuzzy Bag and find no more.

Not long ago, a young woman with big hips born under the sign of Aquarius came to this unhappy land. She seemed not to have heard about the bad witch and was not worried about running out of Warm Fuzzies. She gave them out freely, even when not asked. They called her the Hip Woman and disapproved of her because she was giving the children the idea that they should not worry about running out of Warm Fuzzies. The children liked her very much because they felt good around her and they began to give out Warm Fuzzies whenever they felt like it.

The grownups became concerned and decided to pass a law to protect the children from depleting their supplies of Warm Fuzzies. The law made it a criminal offense to give out Warm Fuzzies in a reckless manner, without a license. Many children, however, seemed not to care; in spite of the law they continued to give each other Warm Fuzzies whenever they felt like it and always when asked. Because there were many, many children, almost as many as grownups, it began to look as if maybe they would have their way.

As of now it is hard to say what will happen. Will the grownup forces of law and order stop the recklessness of the children? Are the grownups going to join with the Hip Woman and the children in taking the chance that there will always be as many Warm Fuzzies as needed? Will they remember the days their children are trying to bring back when Warm Fuzzies were abundant because people gave them away freely?

What the Bible Says About It...

Honor the Lord with thy substance, and with the first fruits of all thine increase: So shall thy barns be filled with plenty, and thy presses shall burst out with new wine. **Proverbs 3:9-10 KJV**

There is one who gives liberally, yet he grows richer, and one who withholds what he should give, and suffers want. The charitable soul shall be enriched, and he who waters, will himself be watered. **Proverbs 11:24,25 MLB**

Bring the whole tithe into the storehouse, so there may be food in My house, and by this put Me to the test, says the Lord of hosts, if I will not open the windows of heaven for you and pour out for you a more than sufficient blessing. **Malachi 3:10-12 MLB**

Cast thy bread upon the waters: for thou shalt find it after many days. **Ecclesiastes 11:1 KJV**

(Rather) is not this the fast that I have chosen: to loose the bonds of wickedness, to undo the bands of the yoke, to let the oppressed go free, and that you break every enslaving yoke? Is it not to divide your bread with the hungry and bring the homeless poor into your house — when you see the naked, that you cover him, and that you hide not yourself from (the needs of) your own flesh and blood? Then shall your light break forth like the morning, and your healing (your restoration and the power of a new life) spring forth speedily; your righteousness (your rightness, your justice, and your right relationship with God) shall go before you (conducting you to peace and prosperity), and the glory of the Lord shall be your rear guard. Then you shall call, and the Lord will answer; you shall cry, and He will say, Here I am. If you take away from your midst yokes of oppression (wherever you find them), the finger pointed in scorn (toward the oppressed or the godly), and every form of false, harsh, unjust, and wicked speaking, And if you pour out that with which you sustain your own life for the hungry and satisfy the need of the afflicted, then shall your light rise in darkness, and your obscurity and gloom become like the noonday. And the Lord shall guide you continually and satisfy you in drought and in dry places and make strong your bones. And you shall be like a watered garden and like a spring of water whose waters fail not. **Isaiah 58:6-11 AB**

So, then, whatever you desire that others would do to and for you, even so do also to and for them, for this is (sums up) the Law and the Prophets. **Matthew 7:12 AB**

Freely you have received; freely give. **Matthew 10:8 MLB**

Give as freely as you have received! **Matthew 10:8 LB**

You received without paying, give without pay. **Matthew 10:8 RSV**

For if you give, you will get! Your gift will return to you in full and overflowing measure, pressed down, shaken together to make room for more, and running over. Whatever measure you use to give — large or small — will be used to measure what is given back to you. **Luke 6:38 LB**

The King will then say to those at his right, "Come, My Father's blessed ones, inherit the kingdom that has been prepared for you from the foundation of the world; for I was hungry and you gave Me food; I was thirsty and you gave Me drink; I was a stranger and you entertained Me; naked, and you clothed Me; sick, and you looked after Me; in prison, and you visited Me." Then the righteous will answer Him "Lord, when did we see You hungry and nourished you, or thirsty and provided You drink? When did we see You a stranger and entertained You, or naked and provided You with clothing? When did we see You ill or in prison and visited You?" And the King will answer, "I assure you, insofar as you did it to one of the least of these brothers of Mine, you did it to Me." **Matthew 25:34-40 MLB**

But when you practice charity, your left hand must not know what your right hand is doing, so that your charity will be in secret. And your Father who sees in secret will reward you openly. **Matthew 6:3,4 AB**

Remember this: he who sows sparingly and grudgingly will also reap sparingly and grudgingly, and he who sows generously that blessings may come to someone will also reap generously and with blessings. Let each one give as he has made up his own mind and purposed in his heart, not reluctantly or sorrowfully or under compulsion, for God loves (He takes pleasure in, prizes above other things, and is unwilling to abandon or to do without) a cheerful (joyous, "prompt to do it") giver whose heart is in his giving. And God is able to make all grace (every favor and earthly blessing) come to you in abundance ... And God Who provides seed for the sower and bread for eating will also provide and multiply your resources for sowing and increase the fruits of your righteousness .... Thus you will be enriched in all things and in every way ... **II Corinthians 9: 6,7,8,10 AB**

Every one must make up his own mind as to how much he should give. Don't force anyone to give more than he really wants to, for cheerful givers are the ones God prizes. God is able to make it up to you by giving you everything you need and more, so that there will not only be enough for your own needs, but plenty left over to give joyfully to others. It is as the Scriptures say: "The godly man gives generously to the poor. His good deeds will be an honor to him forever." (Psalm 112:9) For God, who gives seed to the farmer to plant, and later on, good crops to harvest and eat, will give you more and more seed to plant and will make it grow so that you can give away more and more fruit from your harvest. Yes, God will give you much so that you can give away much ... **II Corinthians 9:7-11 LB**

As for the rich in this world, charge them not to be proud and arrogant and contemptuous of others, nor to set their hopes on uncertain riches, but on God, Who richly and ceaselessly provides us with everything for (our) enjoyment. (Charge them) to do good, to be rich in good works, to be liberal and generous of heart, ready to share (with others), in this way laying up for themselves (the riches that endure forever as) a good foundation for the future, so that they may grasp that which is life indeed. **I Timothy 6:17-19 AB**

But if any one has the world's goods and sees his brother in need, yet closes his heart against him, how does God's love abide in him? **I John 3:17 RSV**

Do not be negligent in showing hospitality, for in doing so some entertained angels without knowing it. **Hebrews 13:2 MLB**

Abbreviations:
AB = Amplified Bible
KJV = King James Version
LB = Living Bible
MLB = Modern Language Bible
RSV = Revised Standard Version
RSV = Revised Standard Version

Chapter 4: The Power of Forgiving Yourself and Others

"Resentment is like taking poison and expecting the other person to die."
— unknown wise person

This lesson, in itself, can completely transform your life if you are willing. So let this lesson (and ALL of the lessons) speak to the part of you that is willing to change.

Again, let's review our definition of prosperity: **"Prosperity is the continuous process of joyfully receiving an abundance of all that we need and joyfully giving back from the overflow."**

Do you get the image of a continuous circulation of GOOD coming TO you, flowing THROUGH you to bless you, and flowing back out into the Universe to bless others? GOOD!

If you can get this image clearly, then you can surely see how guilt, shame, blame, hurt, and resentments within you could block the flow of prosperity to you and through you. So part of our work, then, if we are to attract and receive abundant prosperity into our lives, is to release old hurts, resentments, shame and guilt that no longer serves us — a process also called forgiveness.

Remember that **the purpose of forgiveness is to take back your power.** As long as your energy is being drained by guilt and resentments you will not have the power to create the life you want.

I expect everyone who uses this book has been told at one time or another that they "should" forgive. I also expect that very few have ever been told how to do forgiveness work. Well, I'm about to tell you HOW — in simple terms that anyone can use and understand. There is nothing magic to it — except the results! The only requirements are willingness and a conscious decision to release and clear out old, negative energy so that something new, fresh, and life-affirming can flow into that space.

I am sure some of you are thinking something like, "But I only wanted more MONEY in my life. I never intended to get into all of this!" I would say there is a part of you that wants ALL OF THIS, or you would not be reading and using this workbook.

> As long as your energy is being drained by guilt and resentments you will not have the power to create the life you want.

Forgiving Self

First of all, let's discuss the business of forgiving SELF. Let us start by clarifying the difference between guilt and shame.

Guilt is feeling bad about something I did. Shame is feeling bad about who I am.

Guilt says, "I made a mistake." Shame says, "I AM a mistake."

Guilt actually can serve a useful, short-term purpose. When I violate my own sense of integrity, when I violate my own moral code, healthy guilt tells me immediately that I have messed up — that I am off the true pathway. It is like a signal light that tells me to make a mid-course correction immediately. If I listen to this healthy guilt I can make my correction, get back on course, and make amends or restitution for any harm I have done. At that point, the healthy guilt has served its purpose and then can be released.

Neurotic guilt hangs on, punishing and poisoning indefinitely. It serves no useful purpose.

Every human being I have ever known has done things he or she later regrets. It is part of the human experience. The healthy process is to:

1. admit our mistakes,
2. make corrections,
3. make amends or restitution when possible,
4. learn or re-learn the lesson(s) available,
5. let go of the guilt, and
6. move forward.

Remember that in forgiving you are not condoning the mistake(s) you or others made. You are not saying, "It's OK that this happened." Instead you are saying, **"I am willing to release the pain of the past so that I can be free today."**

It sounds simple, doesn't it? It is simple. It is not necessarily easy — many simple things are not easy. *It is as difficult as we make it.*

This process may be difficult for some of us because we have never seen it modeled. Unfortunately, this simple process is not widely understood or practiced in our culture. What is more commonly practiced is the neurotic, hanging-on kind of self-sabotaging guilt that serves only to keep a person stuck in poverty, pain, and self-imposed victimhood.

The good news is that ANYONE can learn to USE healthy guilt in a constructive, life-enhancing way and then LET GO OF IT! Like everything else, it gets easier with practice.

Unlike guilt, shame serves no useful purpose. Shame is a lie. It says to us, "You're worthless. You're not good enough. You're inadequate. You're stupid, fat, and ugly. You're a mistake. You're bad. You're evil. You don't deserve anything good. You deserve to suffer and to be miserable." And on and on and on.

We live in a shame-based culture. All of our institutions (schools, churches, workplaces, government, families) reinforce shaming ideas and perfectionistic standards that no human can attain. So every human I have ever known has had internalized shame that needed to be released and healed.

Again, the good news is that shame can be released. As conscious adults, we can learn to live in the Truth. The Truth about us is that we are ALL spiritual beings on a human journey. We ARE good enough! We are precious, lovable, and valuable WITHOUT CONDITION. We deserve every good thing the Universe provides for us.

Again, you might say, "But it's not that simple!" I say, "It IS that simple!" And releasing shame is absolutely necessary if we are ever to have abundant prosperity in our lives.

I also would say that releasing internalized shame is typically a process, not an event — it can take time. If so, that's fine. There's plenty of time. Often people doing shame-release work need lots of loving support. If so, that's fine, too. There is LOTS of loving support available.

Survivors of child abuse and/or neglect, people recovering from addictions, women, people of color, differently abled people, people of size, and gay people often need an extra measure of support. That's only because they usually have been given an extra measure of shaming! If that is the case, that's no problem. There is EXTRA support available to anyone who is willing to receive it.

The temptation with forgiveness work is to avoid it, to skip it, or to make cursory, superficial efforts that have no real results. Of course these are options for anyone. I encourage you to take your forgiveness work seriously and to make a sincere effort to be completely honest and thorough. The results will be worth the effort. I guarantee it!

You may be wondering, "Do I have to be 100 percent free from all of my old guilt and shame before I can enjoy prosperity?" The answer is no. Again, the 51 percent rule applies. When 51 percent of your guilt and shame are released, you will notice a significant increase in the flow of prosperity into your life. Of course, you will want to continue that healing process, but be assured that your forgiveness process does not have to be perfectly complete in order for you to enjoy abundant good in your life.

Now I want to offer you a practical tool that is very effective in the process of releasing shame and guilt. The tool is called inventory work. This is one of the very valuable tools I learned in twelve-step recovery work for my addictions. Whether or not you are challenged with addictions, remember that our goal here is to clear away old guilt, shame, and resentment that may be blocking the flow of good into your life. Inventory work is an excellent way to do that. Here is what you do...

Exercises

♥ Journal writing assignment: In your journal, write down EVERYTHING you feel guilt, regret, embarrassment, or shame about. Go back to your earliest memories and write down everything you can recall that you feel any guilt about. Just the facts will do. (Note: Depending on your particular history, it may be very important to write about any sexual behavior you feel guilty, embarrassed, or ashamed about. If this is the case, just do it. In this culture, almost all of us have some healing to do in this area.)

This assignment may be completed in one sitting, over several days, or over several weeks. The point is to get your journal, get a pen, get honest, and get started. Once you have started, write *something* on this assignment at least once a week until it is completed.

As you write you may, at times, begin to feel flooded or overwhelmed with feelings. If this should happen, pause for a moment, breathe deeply, remind yourself that these feelings are coming up to be released and healed, breathe some more, and continue. If tears come, let them flow. Tears are a gift for cleansing.

Breathe through and release any painful energy that comes to the surface as you write. Remember, the writing is not causing the pain. The writing only brings the pain to the surface into your conscious awareness. The pain has been there for a long time. If it were going to kill you, you already would be dead! Feeling it and releasing it is part of healing.

Remember that pain is not your enemy. If you allow it to be, pain can be your teacher and your motivator. Keep writing until you honestly feel complete.

♥ Inventory started on:____/____/____ (date) and completed on ____/____/____ (date).

Now for the next step of releasing guilt and learning to forgive yourself.

♥ It is important for you to share what you have written with at least one other person. You can carefully choose the person you trust to be your listener. It may be your prosperity partner(s), but it also could be a minister, a therapist, a friend, or someone in twelve-step recovery. It is important that the listener be non-judgmental and willing to commit to keeping the information confidential. Ideally, your listener will be a person who has completed a similar process themselves. This also needs to be a person who is comfortable giving affirmation and support.

♥ **To Do:** When you have finished writing this assignment, schedule a time to meet personally with your trusted listener. Allow plenty of time and create a setting where you will not be interrupted or distracted. Read your assignment to your listener, again remembering that any pain you experience in doing this is coming up to be released and healed. Keep breathing and keep reading until you are complete.

♥   As you review your writing assignment with your listener, look for people you may need to make amends to or make restitution to. (Probably the first person you need to make amends to is yourself.) Amends, or restitution, can take the form of a sincere apology, actual monetary payments, or regularly sending positive energy to the person until you feel free. Often the most effective and meaningful amends are "living amends," i.e., changing the way you live in such a way that you are no longer harming yourself or others, and therefore no longer need to feel guilty.

When you are finished reading your assignment to your listener, ask your listener to give you some affirmation and support for your work. You may or may not choose to create a ritual with your listener to symbolize your letting go of the pain of the past. It can be as simple as burning pages of inventory work — or having a pitcher of water and basin nearby where you can symbolically wash your hands.

♥   This writing/reading assignment completed with

_____(name of listener) on ____/____/____ (date).

♥   Journal writing assignment: **In your journal, date an entry and write about this writing/reading assignment. What did you become aware of, learn or relearn by doing it? How do you feel now that it is complete? Discuss with your prosperity partner(s).**

Discussed on: ____/____/____ (date).

♥   Journal writing assignment: **After discussing this with your trusted listener, make a list in your journal of the persons you feel you need to make amends to. Beside each name, write down what form the amends will take, and write down a target date for making each amends. Be sure that any amends you make will not cause harm to yourself or any other person. Report to your prosperity partner(s) how you are doing with making your amends by your target dates. It is OK to revise your target dates if you have unavoidable delays, but don't procrastinate unnecessarily.**

♥   **Amends process started on____/____/____ (date) and completed on____/____/____ (date).**

♥ **Journal Writing Assignment: Date and write an entry about the amends process. What did you become aware of, learn or relearn while making amends? Discuss with your prosperity partner(s).**

Discussed on: ____/____/____ (date).

♥ **To Do:** If you have had the courage and commitment to complete this step of your process, you deserve a reward and/or a celebration. Give yourself one! It may or may not be something you buy. Go inside and ask the part of you that knows, "what would be a fitting reward and celebration for this awesome healing work I am doing?" Keep asking and listen for the answer. Then do it! It may be an afternoon or a morning off to do nothing. It may be a beautiful certificate of achievement you create for yourself. It may be a long-distance phone call to someone special whose voice you haven't heard in awhile. It may be a bouquet of your favorite flowers. Whatever it is, just be sure it is something that nurtures and affirms you.

♥ Describe your celebration and/or reward:

_____

_____

♥ Date of your celebration/reward: ____/____/____ .

NOTE: The previous exercise in doing inventory work is useful for healing guilt AND shame. Most of us decide that if we have made mistakes or done some things that we feel guilty about, then we must be bad people and we feel ashamed. Sharing our guilt list with a non-judgmental, supportive person and making amends helps us to release guilt AND also helps us to see ourselves as human rather than bad.

To further heal our toxic shame, we continue to affirm the truth about ourselves, knowing that we are spiritual beings on a human journey, that we are innately lovable, valuable and precious. We ACT AS IF we believe that until we do! Other pieces of this process also help to address internalized shame issues. Hang in there!

Now on to the next step of your forgiveness process.

Forgiving Others

First of all — *you have a right to be mad, sad and/or hurt.* If anyone has ever abused you, cheated you, neglected you, abandoned you, lied to you, discriminated against you, or hurt you or someone you love in any way, *you have a right to feel whatever you feel about that.* No doubt about it.

> You do not have to carry old (useless) anger with you forever.

In some circumstances, anger is a very reasonable and sane response. Anger energy can be used to create necessary positive change. Once the positive changes are made, however, the remaining anger energy can be harmlessly released. Anger held onto creates resentments. And resentments can poison a person's soul — can absolutely destroy any chance of ever experiencing joyful abundance and prosperity in your life.

The good news — you do not have to carry old (useless) anger with you forever. Anger and resentment can be harmlessly released so that the energy of love and peace and prosperity can flow into your being, healing any old hurts where the anger used to be. Again, in releasing anger and hurt (also known as forgiving) we are NOT saying the hurtful thing that happened should have happened, or that it's OK that it happened, or that you deserved to be hurt. In forgiving, you are simply saying, **"I am willing to release the pain, the anger, the hurt, in order to allow peace and prosperity to flow into my life."**

Again, releasing old anger is typically a process, not an event. It may take time. If it does, that's OK. Again, the 51 percent rule applies. When 51 percent of your resentments are released and healed, miracles will begin to happen in your life. I guarantee it!

The key to releasing your anger is this: In order for the anger to be released it must first be felt and expressed. Too often, we are told to forgive but we are given no permission or support for fully feeling and expressing our pain. I am here to support you in feeling and expressing your anger so that it can be harmlessly released.

Exercises

Here's what you do:

♥ Journal writing assignment: **In your journal, make a list of everyone you can remember who has ever hurt or angered you. Write down their names and what they did. Your list also may include groups of people or institutions. Maybe your list will include God. Put that down — believe me, God can handle it. Maybe your list will include a disease or a natural disaster. Often family members — parents, siblings, ex- or current spouses, in-laws, our children — perhaps the people we cherish and love most — will be at or near the top of the list. Your list may include people who are now deceased. Whoever or whatever you are angry about, put it on the list.**

♥ **As you write, breathe and release. If tears come, let them flow. There is no need to be afraid of any painful feelings that may come to the surface as your write. If these feelings were bad enough to kill you, you already would be dead. Breathe and release and write. Keep writing until you honestly feel complete.**

♥ **This list written on : ____/____/____ (date).**

♥ **When you have finished your list, go back through it and underline or circle five or six names/items that seem to have the most emotional charge for you.**

♥ **Journal writing assignment: Choose one of the names/entities that you have circled or underlined. In your journal, date and begin to write a letter to that person/institution/entity. Do not edit, judge or censor the letter in any way. (You will NOT be sending it!). Let your feelings pour out onto the paper. Use profanity if it comes to mind. (Someone said, "Profanity is the poetry of anger, and we all need poetry.") Be thorough in describing everything that the person/entity did that you feel angry about.**

Again, breathe and release as you write. If you find yourself feeling VERY angry, GREAT! The anger has always been there, outside of your conscious awareness. As you become aware of it you can release it. Have a bath towel close by. If you wish, you can pick up the bath towel and start wringing it into knots, voicing your anger as you do so. Punch a pillow if you need to. If you feel like screaming, scream into a pillow. This will help to release the anger without alarming the neighbors! Another great technique is to take ice cubes out to the sidewalk or to the concrete patio. Hurling the ice cubes and watching them shatter can be an excellent release — as good as breaking dishes — but there is no mess to clean up afterward. Taking a brisk walk also can help to release repressed energy. As you walk, breathe and blow out anger.

Some of this may seem weird or silly. Who's watching? Some of you may be thinking, "What if I lose control and go crazy?" Not a chance. If you were going to lose control or go crazy you would have done so long ago. Your inner wisdom has protected and preserved you and will continue to do so.

Continue your writing, taking whatever breaks you need to take to release old anger energy that comes to the surface.

After thoroughly reviewing the things that the person/entity has done to hurt or anger you and thoroughly expressing ALL of your feelings about that, write something like this if you are ready to do so:

"I am no longer willing to give you power in my life. I am no longer willing to carry hurt and anger because of what you did. I survived you. I release you to your highest good. I forgive you. I bless you. You have no more power in my life."

If you are NOT willing to take the above step — to totally release those who have hurt or angered you — complete the following statement and add it to the letter:

"I am not yet willing to release you. I will continue to give you power to damage and diminish my life. I will continue to carry my anger and hurt for at least another (specific period of time — days, weeks, months or years)."

Close the letter in the way that feels appropriate.

First releasing/forgiving letter written on: ____/____/____ (date).

♥   **If you did not reach the point of releasing, continue to write at least one letter a week to this person/entity until you are willing to completely release.**

♥   Schedule time with a trusted listener. Share the letter with your listener. Ask your listener for affirmation and support for the work you are doing. If you wish, create a simple (or elaborate!) ritual to symbolize your healing and new freedom.

First letter shared with trusted listener on: ____/____/____ (date).

♥   Continue your writing and sharing with your listener until you have written letters to at least five of the people on your list of people who have hurt and/or angered you. Be sure these are the people who have hurt/angered you the MOST.

♥   Additional letters written/shared on (dates):
   2. Date written: ____/____/____ and date shared: ____/____/____
   3. Date written: ____/____/____ and date shared: ____/____/____
   4. Date written: ____/____/____ and date shared: ____/____/____
   5. Date written: ____/____/____ and date shared: ____/____/____

You can share two or more letters with your trusted listener on the same date, if you choose.

If at any time during this process you feel that having the support of a professional therapist would be helpful to you, get it. This is deep, transformative work. In our culture, the professionals who witness and support transformative work are most often mental health professionals. Just be sure, if you seek the support of a therapist, that the therapist is comfortable facilitating anger-release work and be sure that the therapist has done his/her own anger-release work.

If you write letters to the five or six people who have been most hurtful or anger-provoking in your life and share those letters with a trusted listener, you will then have the skills, strength, insight, and maturity to continue and complete your forgiveness work. If you need to write more letters, you will know how to do that. Go inside and ask the part of you that knows for guidance.

By the way, this letter-writing process also is very helpful in resolving grief issues. If you have had significant losses in your life, writing letters and reading them to a trusted listener can help you move through the grief process to acceptance and serenity.

♥ **To Do:** If you have given this work your best, it is time to create another celebration and/or give yourself another reward. Go inside and ask the part of you that knows for guidance in creating your reward/celebration. Then do it!

♥ Describe this second celebration or reward:

_____

_____

_____

♥ Date of your celebration/reward: ___/___/___

As a bonus I have one more forgiveness tool I want to share with you. Again, this comes directly from twelve-step recovery literature, specifically the "Big Book" of *Alcoholics Anonymous*. Page 552 of the "Big Book" suggests:

> *"If you have a resentment you want to be free of, if you will pray for the person or the thing that you resent, you will be free. If you will ask in prayer for everything you want for yourself to be given to them, you will be free. Ask for their helth, their prosperity, their happiness, and you will be free. Even when you don't really want it for them, and your prayers are only words and you don't mean it, go ahead and do it anyway. Do it every day for two weeks and you will find you have come to mean it and to want it for them, you will realize that where you used to feel bitterness and resentment and hatred, you now feel compassionate understanding and love."*

I have used this tool with excellent results, and I highly recommend it. It works really well along with the other tools recommended in this chapter. Even if you do not believe in prayer, you can visualize the person, institution, or entity and send positive energy and good will.

I hope that by this point in our process you have begun to experience forgiveness as a self-empowerment process. Again, **forgiveness is about taking back your power — the power to create the life you want and deserve.**

Affirmations

My feelings are holy, and I honor them.

I am completely forgiven, and I forgive myself for any previous mistakes.

I learn from my mistakes, and I move forward in my journey in joy and freedom.

I completely forgive others. I am learning to understand everyone and everything around me as my teacher.

I forgive myself and others all debts, and I trust my inner wisdom to show me the way.

As I release the past, the new and fresh and vital enter. I allow life to flow through me to bless me and others.

I declare peace and harmony indwell me and surround me at all times. All is well.

Forgiveness is my daily business, and I am faithful in doing my release work.

I trust that right action is always taking place in my life. I am at peace.

I willingly release anything within me that is unlike love.

I know that release is magnetic. Through the act of release, I draw to myself my own. I now fully and freely release. I loose and let go. I let go and grow. I let go and trust. I now let go worn-out things, conditions, and relationships. Divine order is now established and maintained in me and in my world.*

All that has offended me, I forgive. Within and without, I forgive. Things past, things present, things future, I forgive. I forgive everything and everybody who can possibly need forgiveness of the past or present. I forgive positively everyone. I am free and they are free, too. All things are cleared up between us now and forever.*

*(*from the writings of Catherine Ponder, Palm Desert, California, 1971)*

From My Prosperity Scrapbook

My Friend, The Enemy
By the Dalai Lama

"One of my close friends spent, I think, eighteen years in Chinese prison and labor camps. In the early '80s they allowed him to come to India. On occasion he and I discussed his experiences in various Chinese labor camps. And he told me that during those periods, on a few occasions he really faced some danger. I asked what kind of danger, and his response was, 'Oh, danger of losing compassion for the Chinese.' That kind of mental attitude is, I think, a key factor to sustain peace of mind."

His Holiness The Dalai Lama is the spiritual leader of Tibet
Story from an interview for Spirituality and Health,
Winter edition, 1999, with T. George Harris

Words written in a concentration camp

When a Nazi concentration camp was liberated, this prayer by a Jew was found on a scrap of paper:

Peace be to men of bad will, and an end to all revenge and to all words of pain and
   punishment ...
So many have borne witness with their blood!
O God, do not put their suffering upon the scales of Thy justice,
Lest it be counted to the hangman, lest he be brought to answer for his atrocities.
But to all hangmen and informers, to all traitors and evil ones, do grant the benefit of the
   courage and fortitude shown by those others, who were their victims ...
Grant the benefit of the burning love and sacrifice in those harrowed, tortured hearts, which
   remained strong and steadfast in the face of death and unto their weakest hour.
All this, O Lord, may it count in Thine eyes, so that their sin be forgiven.
May this be the ransom that restores justice.
And all that is good, let it be counted, and all that is evil, let it be wiped out...
May peace come once more upon the earth, peace to men of good will, and may it descend
   upon the others also. Amen.

From Dimanche, *a French weekly,*
printed in a pamphlet on forgiveness
published by "The Christophers," New York, NY

"To forgive someone doesn't mean that they were right and you were wrong.
It is simply disconnecting yourself from the incident that caused you distress."
— *Tolly Burkan*, Guiding Yourself into a Spiritual Reality

I first heard a version of the following story many years ago on a tape set recorded by Keith Miller, an Episcopal layman who has authored a number of books on spiritual growth. This is my version of the story.

In her personal prayer and meditation time a woman beheld a glorious vision of the Christ, who spoke words of peace and love to her. A few days later she met with her weekly prayer group and shared with them the miraculous news. It happened that the wife of her minister was a part of her prayer group. The minister's wife went home and told her husband about the woman's vision.

The minister was quite concerned. He had never seen a vision, but he had been to college and had taken a course in abnormal psychology. He had studied about people who saw things and heard things that other people did not see and hear. He called the woman and asked her to come and visit him in his study. She did as he requested.

The minister questioned her, "I understand you saw a vision of Christ and that he spoke to you."

"Yes, pastor, it was a glorious experience," she answered, beaming.

"How do you know it was really Christ?"

"Oh, pastor," she said. "I know! There is no doubt in my mind. The Bible tells us that Jesus said, 'My sheep know my voice.' I'm certain it was the Christ."

"Well, sister," placated the minister, "you know you have to be really careful about these things. I'll tell you what. If you should ever see or speak to this vision again, I want you to ask him a question. Ask him what my worst sin was before I became a minister. This sin is known only to Christ. If it is truly Christ, he will know the answer."

The woman agreed to do as her pastor had instructed and left.

A few days later she returned, excited and anxious to speak to the minister. As soon as she was in his office she blurted out, "Pastor, I saw him! I saw him again! And I spoke to him. Just as you told me to do. I asked him what was your worst sin before you became a minister."

"And what did he say?" the minister interrogated her.

"He said he doesn't remember."

Techniques of Forgiveness

The technique of forgiveness is simple enough, and not very difficult to manage when you understand how. The only thing that is essential is willingness to forgive. Provided you desire to forgive the offender, the greater part of the work is already done. People have always made such a bogey of forgiveness because they have been under the erroneous impression that to forgive a person means that you have to compel yourself to like him. Happily this is by no means the case — we are not called upon to like anyone whom we do not find ourselves liking spontaneously, and indeed, it is quite impossible to like people to order. You can no more like to order than you can hold the winds in your fist, and if you endeavor to coerce yourself into doing so, you will finish by disliking or hating the offender more than ever. ... We are not obliged to like anyone, but we are under a binding obligation to love everyone, love, or charity as the Bible calls it, meaning a vivid sense of impersonal good will. This has nothing directly to do with the feelings, though it is always followed, sooner or later, by a wonderful feeling of peace and happiness.

The method of forgiving is this: Get by yourself and become quiet. Repeat any prayer or treatment that appeals to you, or read a chapter of the Bible. Then quietly say, "I fully and freely forgive X (mentioning the name of the offender); I loose him and let him go. I completely forgive the whole business in question. As far as I am concerned, it is finished forever. I cast the burden of resentment upon the Christ within me. He is free now, and I am free, too. I wish him well in every phase of his life. That incident is finished. The Christ Truth has set us both free. I thank God." Then get up and go about your business. On no account repeat this act of forgiveness because you have done it once and for all, and to do it a second time would be tacitly to repudiate your own work. Afterward, whenever the memory of the offender or the offense happens to come into your mind, bless the delinquent briefly and dismiss the thought. Do this, however many times the thought may come back. After a few days it will return less and less often, until you forget altogether. Then, perhaps after an interval, shorter or longer, the old trouble may come back to memory once more, but you will find that now all bitterness and resentment have disappeared, and you are both free with the perfect freedom of the children of God. Your forgiveness is complete.

— *Emmett Fox,* The Sermon on the Mount, *pp. 189 – 191*

A man went to play golf with his friend Harry. He left home early in the morning. It was almost midnight when he returned. He walked through the door and his wife sarcastically said, "And I suppose you've been playing golf all this time."

"That's right," he replied. "Harry had a massive heart attack on the very first tee and he died. All day and all night it's been hit the ball and drag Harry."

As long as we fail to forgive we are dragging the past, the person, and the incident every moment of every day. We are in effect "dragging Harry." It's time to forgive, "leave Harry" and play on through.

— *Bert Carson,* Daily Inspiration, *October 23, 2000*
http://www.remember-thebook.com/dailyinspiration.htm

"One of my teachers had each one of us bring a clear plastic bag and a sack of potatoes. For every person we'd refuse to forgive in our life experience, we were told to choose a potato, write on it the name and date, and put it in the plastic bag. Some of our bags, as you can imagine, were quite heavy.

We were then told to carry this bag with us everywhere for one week, putting it beside our bed at night, on the car seat when driving, next to our desk at work. The hassle of lugging this around with us made it clear what a weight we were carrying spiritually, and how we had to pay attention to it all the time to not forget, and keep leaving it in embarrassing places.

Naturally, the condition of the potatoes deteriorated to a nasty slime. This was a great metaphor for the price we pay for keeping pain and heavy negativity! Too often we think of forgiveness as a gift to the other person, and it clearly is for ourselves!!

So the next time you decide you can't forgive someone, ask yourself...isn't your bag heavy enough?"

— *Author Unknown*

One ex-prisoner of war asked another, "Have you forgiven your captors yet?"
The second one replied, "No, never."
And the other turned and said, "Then it seems they still have you in prison, don't they?"

What the Bible Says About It...

Make me, Your servant, to rejoice, O Lord, for to You do I lift myself up. For You, O Lord, are good, and ready to forgive (our trespasses, sending them away, letting them go completely and forever); and You are abundant in mercy and loving-kindness to all those who call upon You. **Psalms 86: 4,5 AB**

I bless the holy name of God with all my heart. Yes, I will bless the Lord and not forget the glorious things he does for me. He forgives all my sins. He heals me. He ransoms me from hell. He surrounds me with loving kindness and tender mercies. He fills my life with good things. My youth is renewed like the eagle's. **Psalms 103: 1-5 LB**

As far as the east is from the west, so far has He removed our transgressions from us. **Psalms 103:12 MLB**

For if you forgive people their trespasses (their reckless and willful sins, leaving them, letting them go, and giving up resentment) your heavenly Father will also forgive you. But if you do not forgive others their trespasses (their reckless and willful sins, leaving them, letting them go, and giving up resentment), neither will your Father forgive you your trespasses. **Matthew 6:14-15 AB**

Then came Peter to him, and said, Lord, how oft shall my brother sin against me, and I forgive him? till seven times? Jesus saith unto him, I say not unto thee, Until seven times: but: Until seventy times seven. **Matthew 18:21, 22 KJV**

Judge not, (neither pronouncing judgment nor subjecting to censure), and you will not be judged; do not condemn and pronounce guilty, and you will not be condemned and pronounced guilty; acquit and forgive and release (give up resentment, let it drop), and you will be acquitted and forgiven and released. **Luke 6: 37 AB**

Therefore, since we are justified (acquitted, declared righteous, and given a right standing with God) through faith, let us (grasp the fact that we) have the peace of reconciliation to hold and to enjoy) peace with God through our Lord Jesus Christ (the Messiah, the Anointed One). **Romans 5:1 AB**

There is therefore now no condemnation to them which are in Christ Jesus, who walk not after the flesh, but after the Spirit. **Romans 8:1 KJV**

Who dares accuse us whom God has chosen for his own? Will God? No! He is the one who has forgiven us and given us right standing with himself. **Romans 8:33 LB**

And He will establish you to the end (keep you steadfast, give you strength, and guarantee your vindication: He will be your warrant against all accusation or indictment so that you will be) guiltless and irreproachable in the day of our Lord Jesus Christ (the Messiah). God is faithful (reliable, trustworthy, and therefore ever true to His promise, and He can be depended on); by Him you were called into companionship and participation with His Son, Jesus Christ our Lord. **I Corinthians 1:8,9 AB**

Let all bitterness and indignation and wrath (passion, rage, bad temper) and resentment (anger, animosity) and quarreling (brawling, clamor, contention) and slander (evil-speaking, abusive or blasphemous language) be banished from you, with all malice (spite, ill will, or baseness of any kind). And become useful and helpful and kind to one another, tenderhearted (compassionate, understanding, loving-hearted), forgiving one another, (readily and freely), as God in Christ forgave you. **Ephesians 4:31-32 AB**

Be gentle and ready to forgive; never hold grudges. Remember, the Lord forgave you, so you must forgive others. **Colossians 3:13 LB**

Finally, all of you, have unity of spirit, sympathy, love of the brethren, a tender heart and a humble mind. Do not return evil for evil or reviling for reviling; but on the contrary bless, for to this you have been called, that you may obtain a blessing. **I Peter 3:8,9 RSV**

Above all things have intense and unfailing love for one another, for love covers a multitude of sins (forgives and disregards the offenses of others). **I Peter 4:8 AB**

For if our heart condemn us, God is greater than our heart, and knoweth all things. **I John 3:30 KJV**

Abbreviations:
AB = Amplified Bible
KJV = King James Version
LB = Living Bible
MLB = Modern Language Bible
RSV = Revised Standard Version
RSV = Revised Standard Version

Chapter 5: The Power of Knowing Your True Purpose

"I never thought of achievement. I just did what came along
for me to do — the thing that gave me the most pleasure."
— Eleanor Roosevelt

In our definition of prosperity we agreed that one of the things we all need in order to be prosperous is meaningful work and a sense of purpose in our lives. Other words for true purpose include calling, quest, mission, sending, destiny, assignment, bliss, or passion. The Buddhists teach this principle as the concept of Sumijava, or "right livelihood" or "right living." Hindus teach this as "the Law of Dharma."

Universally, the idea is that **we are each born with unique gifts, talents, aptitudes, predispositions, temperaments, and personalities and with a unique purpose.** We will enjoy peace and prosperity as we discover that purpose and use those gifts to fulfill it. Always, expressing our gifts and fulfilling our purpose not only creates prosperity for us but blesses others as well. As the Universe is enriched by our giving, the Universe gives back to us everything we need.

David Sawyer, director of Students for Appalachia, in Berea, Kentucky, made these remarks to the students at the Berea College Senior Banquet on March 2, 1998:

"The universe rewards the path with heart — a path of action, of service, a path of unending willingness to make things better. … Whatever career you choose, whoever you marry, however it all goes for you, remember to ask yourself the question that you alone can answer — does this path have a heart? … It has become almost inevitable in American society that people will spend much of their productive lives working at a job that is really not their calling, that involves a good deal of pain and struggle, and that rarely, if ever, inspires them. Because of this, we are a nation full of doctors who are not healers, lawyers who do not uphold justice and educators who can't teach. … My favorite phrase for what work ought to be is something called 'right livelihood.' It's the idea that the manner in which you earn your living ought to not only make a contribution to the world, but serve your own character development and higher or spiritual growth, too." (Quoted in the Berea College Alumni Journal, *Spring, 1998 edition.)*

Many of us, instead of finding our true purpose, unconsciously work for money to survive, living for our coffee break, lunch break, quitting time, the weekend, and vacation. Anyone who does this is not enjoying prosperity no matter how much money they earn or how many toys they own.

Part of prosperity, then, is to determine for ourselves what work we will do that will add meaning and joy to our lives and to the lives of others. A prosperous person does not work for money. **Money is a terrible master and a wonderful servant. Money serves the prosperous person.**

Danaan Parry resigned his prestigious position with the Atomic Energy Commission and a few years later founded an international peacekeeping organization called the Earthstewards Network. Danaan tells a story in his book *Warriors of the Heart* about his time working with Mother Teresa in Bombay. She told him to throw out his old ideas about service. She said to him, "True service is doing what fills you up; that which brings you a sense of joyful purpose. It's not doing what 'should' be done, it's doing what you love to do, and doing it with all your heart. And," she said, "you will discover that this is exactly what God intended for you to do."

Danaan believed that right livelihood was essential not only for the individual but also for saving our planet! In a booklet entitled *The Aikido of Livelihood*, he wrote, "Reaching Samajiva (right livelihood) lies within the grasp of every person in America. And all it will take is about 15 percent of us reaching it for an avalanche-effect to occur. That is, a critical mass of about 15 percent will start a geometric expansion, because it will become safe, and acceptable, and even somewhat lucrative, as new sustainable businesses are created and new, more holistic, environmentally aware markets appear. When 15 percent of us are earning our money in congruence with our values and our dreams, the effect on the rest of the planet will be completely noticeable. Our consumption will go way down; our need for diversion (the entertainment and media industries) will be forced to transform to Right Living, violence will significantly decrease, and social awareness, both in America and for the rest of the Earth, will skyrocket. And perhaps most needed, our collective spirit will once again be feeding the Earth, instead of draining it."

The noted scholar, professor, and philosopher Joseph Campbell said, "Follow your bliss. ... When you follow your bliss doors will open where you would not have thought there would be doors; and where there wouldn't be a door for anyone else."

We cannot enjoy prosperity without "following our bliss." So the question becomes, "what is my bliss?" Again I remind you that **there is a part of you that knows everything you need to know.** That part of you knows exactly what work, what goal, what mission can bring you the greatest joy, the greatest fulfillment, the greatest sense of meaning and purpose.

In my Universe, there are no mistakes, no accidents, no coincidences. It is no accident or mistake that you were born. **You were born for a purpose.** Only you can determine for yourself what that purpose might be. I know your purpose is greater than worrying about how to pay your bills. Or worrying about how you will get by if you retire. Or worrying about how you will send your kids to college. Or worrying about money, period.

I choose to believe that all of us spiritual beings on a human journey were born to give and receive love, to experience bliss, and to help and to bless one another. There are infinite creative ways we can choose to realize these purposes.

You may find that the *expression* of your purpose changes over time as you evolve and grow in consciousness. For example, I know that my divine purpose is to learn, live, and teach spiritual truth. Earlier in my life I expressed that purpose through my psychotherapy practice. Since undergoing a process I call mid-life transformation, my bliss is to write, present workshops and retreats, and to provide prosperity coaching and teacher mentoring. My purpose has not changed. The outward expression of my purpose has developed and matured into a new form.

In her book *Fulfill Your Soul's Purpose*, Naomi Stephan, Ph.D., states that "Life is a personal mission. You have a calling that exists only for you and that only you can fulfill. ... Think of Life Mission as the melody, the theme of your life ... career, on the other hand, is the musical instrument you play it on. Using different instruments (careers, avocations, and the like) you can express your mission in varying and interesting ways, but the melody (mission) stays the same. Thus you have infinite possibilities, infinite variations possible within one basic theme."

> "Life is a personal mission. You have a calling that exists only for you and that only you can fulfill...Think of Life Mission as the melody, the theme of your life..."
> — Naomi Stephan, Ph.D.

I do not assume that everyone is called to be a professional helper, or a religious leader, or a public servant. **People can find and follow their bliss in almost any line of work.**

A few years ago I lived in a community where several times a week I drove down a street that had once been a residential area. As the town grew and developed, the zoning had changed in that neighborhood and the small houses were all converted to businesses. One business was devoted exclusively to selling brightly colored decorative banners — the kind that people hang by flagpoles in front of their homes. Near the entrance to the shop the owner displayed at least 25 to 30 of the bright banners. No matter what kind of day I was having, whenever I would drive by that little shop and see all of those gorgeous banners flapping in the breeze I would smile and my heart would lift. I would think, "The person who owns that shop must surely be following their bliss." And I would feel inspired by their example.

My husband and I currently live, work, and travel full-time in our RV. We stay for varying periods of time in many different RV campgrounds. When we pull into a new campground I can tell almost immediately whether the owners/managers of the campground are making a living or following their bliss. The latter can be recognized by the light in their eyes, by the genuine warmth with which they greet their campers, by the little extra touches that communicate their caring. Customer service is their priority. They regularly go the extra mile to make their guests feel welcomed and comfortable. They pay attention to the small details of keeping the campground clean and functional while never losing sight of the larger goal — building lasting friendships.

I have known hair stylists who were absolutely blissed out doing hair. They generally asked for and received very high fees!

For a few very special people, parenting is bliss. For most of us, however, parenting is a temporary extracurricular activity — a very important one, to be sure! For most of us it is not our bliss.

There is no reason to feel guilty if you have children but find you have other interests and passions in your life. Remember that the Universe loves and supports your children just as the Universe loves and supports you. (As Edwene Gaines says, "God doesn't have any grandchildren!")

Please do not misinterpret this as meaning children are not important. Children are extremely important! Whether or not parenting is your bliss, I do believe that parenting is one of the richest learning experiences a person can create for themselves. I also believe that parents can fulfill their rightful responsibilities to their children and also follow their bliss, which may have little to do with their children. In fact, finding a true purpose and following bliss is one of the greatest examples parents can set for their children. (For some readers this is a very significant point. Others will hardly give it notice. If this is a major point for you, write about it in your journal and share your thoughts with your prosperity partner.)

Here's how you know if you are living on purpose: Do you absolutely love what you do? Does time fly when you are at work? Is your work in alignment with your personal values and dreams? Does your work demonstrate, call forth and require the highest and best in you? Does it honor the highest and best in others? Does it stretch you, strengthen you, inspire you, invigorate you? Would you continue to do it if you won the Publisher's Clearinghouse Sweepstakes?

Exercises

♥ **To Do:** Think about the above questions in terms of the work you currently do, and share your answers to these questions with your prosperity partner(s).

Shared on:___/___/____ (date).

In order to enjoy prosperity, I encourage you to consider the question, "What is the true purpose of my life?" Assume that you were born to be joyful, that you were given certain gifts to joyfully express, and that in expressing these gifts you not only find bliss yourself but bring joy and beauty to others. Also, assume that you can passionately pursue this purpose and that the Universe will support you as you do so.

Some of you already know what your bliss/true purpose is. Some have never given it a thought. In either case, I invite you to complete the following awareness exercises. If you think you already know, this will help you clarify your thoughts and intentions. If you've never given it a thought before now, this will begin to give you an idea of your true purpose.

♥ **To Do:** (This project is really fun to do with your prosperity partner(s) or with any small group.) For this exercise you will need a large piece of poster board, scissors, glue, and a variety of old magazines, catalogs, travel brochures, etc. Go through the magazines and other materials and allow yourself to intuitively choose words and pictures that represent or describe the life you would be living if you were following your bliss. Don't think too much. Just let your playful, intuitive, inner Self do the choosing. Cut out the pictures and words and arrange them in a pleasing way on your poster board. Glue them down. This should take no more than about 20 – 30 minutes. Keep your collage in a place where you will see it often. Take a snapshot of it and put the snapshot in your daily planner or tape it in a place where you will see it every day. If you choose, you can create a new collage every six to nine months or once a year.

♥   This assignment completed on:____/____/____ (date).

♥   Share your collage with your prosperity partner(s). Shared on____/____/____ (date).

♥ **Journal writing assignment: Date an entry and write about this: What did you learn or relearn or become aware of as you were making your collage?**

♥ **Share this with your prosperity partner(s).**

Shared on____/____/____ (date).

Suzanne Falter-Barns is a speaker, writer, mother, occasional singer and author of *How Much Joy Can You Stand? A Creative Guide to Facing Your Fears and Making Your Dreams Come True* (Ballantine, 2000). She suggests making the following lists to help you discover what you feel passionate about. She recommends, "Be honest, and keep adding to them as you further discover what moves you."

- "People Whose Permission I Am Waiting For"
- "Things I Loved to Make or Do as a Child"
- "What I Daydream About When Waiting in Lines"
- "Activities That Make Me Feel Spiritually Connected"
- "What I Think About When I'm Alone in Nature"

♥ **Journal writing assignment: In your journal, create your list of "people whose permission you are waiting for." Then choose one or more of the other topics and make lists. Share these lists with your prosperity partner(s).**

Shared on____/____/____ (date).

♥   Just for fun, imagine for a moment that one year ago you received an inheritance so large that you never have to be concerned about money and finances again. The money is now invested in such a way that the interest and dividends create for you a continuous supply of more money than you can possibly spend. You have now acquired your dream home and everything to go with it. You have hired honest, trustworthy assistants to manage your financial assets. Describe in detail how you are spending your time.

_____

_____

_____

♥   Complete these statements. (Remember, if you don't know, make up something!)

To change the world I would like to _____

I am happiest when I_____

Wouldn't it be great if I could _____

Someone with purpose whom I admire is _____

At the age of 95 I would like to look back on my life and say this is what I have accomplished:

_____

I would get satisfaction in my life if I could _____

If I were guaranteed success I would _____

(Adapted from The Joy of Not Working, *by Ernie Zelenski)*

My gifts/talents/aptitudes include:

_____

_____

_____

Note: This is no time for false modesty. Everyone has gifts, talents, and aptitudes. Write yours down! If you have difficulty with this, ask for help from people who know you well. Even if you don't have difficulty, it could be helpful to ask people who know you well what they see as your gifts, talents, and aptitudes. You may be overlooking your own strongest asset.

I have a passion for/intense interest in/fascination for/unlimited energy for:

_____

_____

I want my epitaph to read: _____

I would like to be remembered for: _____

♥   Share your answers with your prosperity partner(s). Shared on ___/___/___ (date).

♥   Since completing these exercises, thinking about it, and discussing it with my prosperity partner(s), I think my true purpose or bliss is:

_____

_____

_____

♥   Now complete this statement: Following my bliss/fulfilling my true purpose would create the following changes in my life:

_____

_____

_____

and I would feel _____

♥   Discussed with partner(s) on: ___/___/___ (date).

(Special note to those who feel that their divine purpose may include teaching prosperity principles to others: If you would be interested in having an experienced mentor to support and guide you as you "follow your bliss," contact me, Grace Terry, at the numbers given on page 127.)

Keeping in mind your true purpose/bliss, now continue on to the next chapter — the power of knowing what you want.

Affirmations

I choose with joy and confidence the meaning and true purpose of my life.

I choose to follow my bliss.

My inner wisdom guides me to the ideal expression of my purpose.

I was born to experience joy, to love and be loved, and to follow my bliss.

I am a uniquely gifted spiritual being, and I joyfully and generously share my gifts with the world.

As I share my gifts with the Universe, following my bliss, the Universe rewards me with unlimited prosperity and abundance.

From My Prosperity Scrapbook

"This is the true joy in life: the being used for a purpose recognized by yourself as a mighty one; the being a force of nature instead of a feverish, selfish little clod of ailments and grievances, complaining that the world will not devote itself to making you happy. My life belongs to the whole community and as long as I live it is my privilege to do for it whatever I can. I want to be thoroughly used up when I die. Life is no brief candle to me. It is a splendid torch which I have got hold of for the moment, and I want to make it burn as brightly as possible before handing it on to future generations."

— *George Bernard Shaw*

"The purpose of life is not to be happy. It is to be useful, to be honorable, to be compassionate, to have it make some difference that you have lived and lived well."

— *Ralph Waldo Emerson*

"Work is love made visible. And if you cannot work with love but only with distaste, it is better that you should leave your work and sit at the gate of the temple and take alms of those who work with joy. For if you bake bread with indifference, you bake a bitter bread that feeds but half our hunger."

— *Kahlil Gibran*

"Everybody can be great … because anybody can serve. You don't have to have a college degree to serve. You don't have to make your subject and verb agree to serve. You only need a heart full of grace. A soul generated by love."

— *Martin Luther King, Jr.*

"I don't know what your destiny will be, but one thing I know: the only ones among you who will be happy are those who have sought and found how to serve."

— *Albert Schweitzer*

"God doesn't call the qualified. God qualifies the called."

— *Unknown*

The following was printed in Sojo Mail — *an e-zine published by* Sojourner's Magazine, *August 2000.*

Pop Quiz:

1. Name the five wealthiest people in the world.
2. Name the last five Heisman trophy winners.
3. Name the last five winners of the Miss America contest.
4. Name ten people who have won the Nobel or Pulitzer prize.
5. Name the last half dozen Academy Award winners for best actor and actress.
6. Name the last decade's worth of World Series winners.

How did you do? The point is, few of us remember the headliners of yesterday. These are no second-rate achievers. They are tops in their fields. But the applause dies. Awards tarnish. Accolades and certificates are buried with their owners.

Here's another quiz. See how you do on this one:
1. List a few teachers who aided your journey through school.
2. Name three friends who have helped you through a difficult time.
3. Name five people who have taught you something worthwhile.
4. Think of a few people who have made you feel appreciated and special.
5. Think of five people you enjoy spending time with.
6. Name half a dozen heroes whose stories have inspired you.

Easier? The lesson...the people who make a difference in your life are not the ones with the most credentials, the most money, or the most awards. They are the ones who care.

"We must be the change we wish to see in the world." — *Gandhi*

Senator Edward Everette, an orator of great renown, was the principle speaker at the dedication of the Gettysburg National Cemetery. He spoke for almost two hours. Abraham Lincoln was added to the program as an after-thought. He spoke for four minutes and twenty seconds. Today no one remembers what Senator Everette said that day at Gettysburg. However, school children for the past 140 years have memorized every word that Abraham Lincoln spoke. Everette was an eloquent speaker. A man who knew the words and how to deliver them. Abraham Lincoln was not an polished speaker. He was the change he wished to see in the world and that made all the difference. It still does.

— *Bert Carson,* Daily Inspiration, *October 24, 2000*
http://www.remember-thebook.com/dailyinspiration.htm

In his book An Inside Job: A Spiritual Approach to Finding Your Right Work, *G. Richard Rieger suggests that seekers meditate on the following questions:*

Beloved Indwelling Spirit, what is my highest aspiration — that which I came to fulfill?
Beloved Indwelling Spirit, what is Your Highest Aspiration for me — that which You would have me fulfill? What do You desire to accomplish through me?
Beloved Indwelling Spirit, what is the first action step You want me to take toward my goal, beginning today?

Richard writes, "Listening to your Intuitive Guide is the secret of finding your way, rather than listening to the voice of the intellect that only confuses you with doubt. Know that your Indwelling Spirit will be working through you and will be providing you with courage, love and all the resources necessary to your success. The entire universe will flow to fill the vessel of your earnest desire, just as the entire ocean flows to fill a hole dug by a small child with a tiny shovel by the edge of the sea. You are that beloved child."

Deepak Chopra is a physician and an international authority on mind/body medicine. His teachings combine physics and philosophy, Eastern wisdom and Western science. In his book Seven Spiritual Laws of Success *he writes:*

"Expressing your talents to fulfill needs creates unlimited wealth and abundance. If you could start children right from the beginning with this thought, you'd see the effect it has on their lives. In fact, I did this with my own children. Again and again, I told them there was a reason why they were here, and they had to find out what that reason was for themselves. From the age of four years, they heard this. I also taught them to meditate when they were about the same age, and I told them, 'I never, ever want you to worry about making a living. If you're unable to make a living when you grow up, I'll provide for you, so don't worry about that. I don't want you to focus on doing well in school. I don't want you to focus on getting the best grades or going to the best colleges. What I really want you to focus on is asking yourself how you can serve humanity, and asking yourself what your unique talents are. Because you have a unique talent that no one else has, and you have a special way of expressing that talent, and no one else has it.' They ended up going to the best schools, getting the best grades, and even in college, they are unique in that they are financially self-sufficient, because they are focused on what they are here to give. This then, is the Law of Dharma."

Matthew Fox, author of many books including The Reinvention of Work, *envisions a world of work where intellect, heart, and health come together to celebrate the whole person. A true teacher of his beliefs, he recreated his career after being dismissed by the Dominican order in 1993. He is now president of the University of Creation Spirituality. In an interview published in* Personal Transformation Journal, *(Anniversary, 2000 issue), Matthew was asked to expand on his idea of the importance of asking what life is calling forth from you. This is his reply:*

"Why are you here? It has taken fifteen billion years to get you here. That is a scientific fact. We are not just the products of our parents. Sixty percent of our body is hydrogen atoms. The hydrogen atoms in us go back to the fireball fourteen billion years ago. We have been around a long time, and it has been a great birthing process to bring us forward. So you have to presume there is some reason for being here, other than going shopping. We have to probe that reason. What are our talents? What is the pain in the world that speaks to us that we want to respond to? What gifts do we have, whether material goods or power to influence? What gifts do we have to make a difference? We are all living under this sword of the collapse of the ecosystem and what are we doing about it? Are we planting trees, are we working to preserve the species that are disappearing or the soil or the forests? Are we cutting back on our addiction to meat, changing our eating habits, using less land, water and grain for our eating habits? Are we being responsible, and how does it come through in our work and in our job?"

For information on Matthew Fox or the Institute of Creation Spirituality, call 510-835-4827 or visit the web-site at www.creationspirituality.com or e-mail ucs@csnet.org.

"Make sure that your life is a rare entertainment! It doesn't take anything drastic. You needn't be gorgeous or wealthy or smart. Just very enthusiastic!"

— *Bette Midler*

The American Dream

The American investment banker was at the pier of a coastal Mexican village when a small boat with just one fisherman docked. Inside the boat were several large yellow fin tuna. The American complimented the Mexican on the quality of his fish and asked how long it took to catch them. The Mexican replied only a little while.

The American asked why didn't he stay out longer and catch more fish. The Mexican said he had enough to support his family's immediate needs.

The American then asked, "but what do you do with the rest of your time?"

The Mexican fisherman said, "I sleep late, fish a little, play with my children, take siesta with my wife Maria, stroll into the village each evening where I sip wine and play guitar with my amigos. I have a full and busy life."

The American scoffed, "I am a Harvard MBA and could help you. You should spend more time fishing and with the proceeds, buy a bigger boat. With the proceeds from the bigger boat you could buy several boats. Eventually you would have a fleet of fishing boats. Instead of selling your catch to a middleman you could sell directly to the processor, eventually opening your own cannery. You would control the product, processing, and distribution. You would need to leave this small village and move to Mexico City, then Los Angeles, and eventually New York City where you will run your expanding enterprise.

The Mexican fisherman asked, "But how long will this all take?"

To which the American replied, "Fifteen to twenty years."

"But what then?"

The American laughed and said, "That's the best part. When the time is right you would announce an IPO and sell your company stock to the public and become very rich. You would make millions!"

"Hmmm. ... Millions. Then what?"

"Then you would retire. Move to a small coastal fishing village where you would sleep late, fish a little, play with your kids, take siesta with your wife, stroll to the village in the evenings where you could sip wine and play guitar with your amigos."

What the Bible Says About It...

For I know the plans I have for you, declares the Lord, plans to prosper you and not to harm you, plans to give you hope and a future. **Jeremiah 29:11 NIV**

I will instruct you (says the Lord) and guide you along the best pathway for your life; I will advise you and watch your progress. **Psalm 32:8 LB**

Trust in the Lord with all thine heart ... In all thy ways acknowledge him, and he shall direct thy paths. **Proverbs 3:5,6 KJV**

Delight yourself also in the Lord, and He will give you the desires and secret petitions of your heart. Commit your way to the Lord (roll and repose each care of your load on Him); trust (lean on, rely on, and be confident) also in Him and He will bring it to pass. **Psalm 37:4,5 AB**

You are the world's seasoning, to make it tolerable. ... You are the world's light — a city on a hill, glowing in the night for all to see. Don't hide your light! Let it shine for all; let your good deeds glow for all to see, so that they will praise your heavenly Father. **Matthew 5:13-16 LB**

But as it is written, eye hath not seen, nor ear heard, neither have entered into the heart of man, the things which God hath prepared for them that love him. **I Corinthians 2:9 KJV**

We are assured and know that (God being a partner in their labor) all things work together and are (fitting into a plan) for good to and for those who love God and are called according to God's design and purpose. **Romans 8:28 AB**

God has given each of you some special abilities; be sure to use them to help each other, passing on to others God's many kinds of blessings. **I Peter 4:10 LB**

Abbreviations:
AB = Amplified Bible
KJV = King James Version
LB = Living Bible
MLB = Modern Language Bible
RSV = Revised Standard Version
RSV = Revised Standard Version

Chapter 6: The Power of Visioning

Knowing What You Want and Going for It!

"The future belongs to those who believe in the beauty of their dreams."
— Eleanor Roosevelt

This chapter will continue the work you began in the previous section on finding your true purpose and following your bliss.

Part of our spiritual work is to get clear with ourselves and with the Universe about what we want. Many of us are less than thrilled with what we have in our lives, but we are not clear about what we want instead. It is not enough to know what we don't want. We must also decide what we do want.

Sometimes we confuse ourselves about what we want. Confusion is what we do to keep ourselves from knowing and taking responsibility. Again, I remind you that **there is a part of you that knows everything you need to know.** When completing the exercises in this section, go inside and ask the part of you that knows for guidance.

One thing that can create confusion about what we want is any lingering doubt about our worthiness. If this is the case with you, here is an excellent opportunity to "act as if." In completing this exercise, you can act as if you deserve to have every good thing you want AND that the Universe wants to give it to you. (If you need help here see Chapter 1.)

Also, act as if you are not willing to settle for anything less than what you want. Remember, *the space for what you want in your life is already filled by what you settled for instead.*

You can decide RIGHT NOW not to settle for less than what you really want.

You also can decide that you are willing to release anything in your life that might prevent you from having everything you want. This might include old ideas, old beliefs, old relationships that do not support your prosperity, the fear of change, or the perceived comfort of the status quo. This also might include giving up all of your old excuses, like "I'm too fat/thin/tall/short/young/old," "I don't have enough/the right education," "my hair is too curly/too straight/red/gray/all gone," "I'm a victim of child abuse/spouse abuse/elder abuse," "my parents/spouse/kids/friends would never understand," "I can't get ahead, I can't get a break," "it would never work out," and on and on and on.

This kind of thinking will get you nothing but the "same old, same old." Are you willing to let go of it for something better?

Remember, *if you always do what you always did, you will always get what you always got.*

Exercises

♥ Journal writing assignment: **In your journal, date an entry and make a list of everything you can imagine you want in your life, keeping in mind your true purpose.** *Make sure everything on your list is concrete and tangible and measurable.* **Write down anything that comes to your mind. If you get blocked, make up something. This exercise can be great fun! Allow your imagination to create an extravagant list! Keep writing until you cannot possibly think of anything else to add to the list.**

♥ Now go back to the list and circle three to five items you want most. (Completing this exercise with a few of the things on your list will teach you how to use this process for manifesting *anything* on your list.)

♥ Take these three to five items and write them down again, this time adding details. For example, if you want more income — decide specifically how much income you want. Calculate a dollar amount per week, per month, or per year. If you want more friends — define the word "friend" — describe in specific detail what the word friend means to you and decide exactly how many more friends you want in your life. What qualities and characteristics will these friends have? What do you see yourself doing with your new friends? If you want a new car, describe the car in great detail. How will it look, feel, smell? How will you feel driving it? If you want a new career, describe the new career with as much detail as possible. Again, in every case, assume and act as if you deserve to have everything you want, that the Universe is unlimited in its supply, and that the Universe wants to give you everything you want.

♥ Go back to the list of three to five items. By each item, write a date by which you would be willing to receive that gift into your life.

Visualization: Go back to the list of three to five items. See yourself achieving these goals. Take each goal in order and imagine yourself achieving that goal. What does it look like when you achieve that goal? What does it smell like and sound like? How does it feel?

♥ Journal writing assignment: **In your journal, describe in detail how it looks, sounds, smells, and feels when you achieve each of these three to five goals. Write this description in the present tense, rather than the future tense. (Example: Today I am driving my brand new car. It is bright red. It smells like leather. The CD player is playing my favorite song. I feel …) Share this description with your prosperity partner(s).**

Shared on: ____/____/____ (date).

♥ Again, go back to the list of three to five items. Beside each item, write down what you must give up or release or transform in order to receive this into your life. For example, if you want more income, you might need to be willing to give up your comfort with poverty or your fear of not being able to handle more income. If you want more friends, you might need to give up the illusion of the comfort and safety of your isolation. If you want a beautiful new car, you might need to give up the false idea that you are unworthy of driving a beautiful new car. If you want a new career, you might need to become willing to give up the rewards and perks of the old one. If you get stumped, go inside and ask the part of you that knows. Talk it over with your partner(s). If all else fails, make up something!

♥ When this detailed list of three to five most wanted, tangible, concrete, measurable items is complete, write at the bottom of the list:

"This is what I want. I know I deserve everything I want. I will not settle for less. I release anything within me that might prevent me from receiving these gifts into my life. I declare these desires to the Universe, knowing that the Universe supports me, and that this or something better is coming to me NOW!"
(Then sign your name.)

This list completed on: ___/___/___ (date).

♥ Share this list with your prosperity partner(s). Read the declaration aloud to your partner(s). Shared with partner(s) on: ___/___/___ (date).

♥ Go back to the list. Beside each item, write down the thing you can do IMMEDIATELY — within the next week — to begin to bring this gift into your life. For instance, suppose you want to start your own business. What can YOU do immediately about that? Perhaps you need to go to the library and find a book on how to write a business plan. Perhaps you need to search for a location for your business. Perhaps you need to call the Chamber of Commerce and ask about its services. Again, let the part of you that knows guide you. Make a list of things to do over the next week. Take small steps in the direction of your dreams. Dr. Martin Luther King, Jr., said,

"Take the first step in faith. You don't have to see the whole staircase, just take the first step."

This list of things to do completed on ___/___/___ (date).

♥ Share this list of things to do with your prosperity partner(s).

Shared with partner(s) on: ___/___/___ (date).

♥   Keep your list of three-to-five most wanted items in a place where you will see it and read it at least twice each day.

♥   In your journal, keep an ongoing list of things to do that will move you in the direction of manifesting all you desire. As you complete each item on your list of things to do, make a check by that item and write the date you completed that task. Continue to share with your prosperity partner(s) your progress toward your goals.

As you take the steps you are capable of taking toward manifesting your desires, expect the Universe to support you. Expect doors to open for you. Expect to find the right information, the right people, the right resources you need in order to be, do, and have all that you desire. Expect to be blessed and to be a blessing to others. Expect miracles! With this attitude, and the other work that you have done in preparation for this step, failure is impossible!

When you hit a brick wall, turn left and keep on going!

For a time it may seem best to continue working at a job that is not necessarily your bliss. If this is the case, I encourage you to do that job with joy and gratitude, even as you make plans for a change. Do whatever you have to do to create a life that is free of other responsibilities so that you can devote yourself full-time to following your bliss. While in the process, be grateful and gracious every day.

As you achieve and attain each goal, add new ones to the list of most wanted goals.

Some of you are thinking, "You mean I have to DO SOMETHING? I have to GIVE UP SOME-THING, my excuses, my b.s., my comfort zone?" Yes, creating prosperity requires you to be willing to change and to step out in confidence in the direction of your dreams. **Once you become fully committed to being, doing, and having all that you want — for every step you take, the Universe will take ten steps to support you.** You may not believe this, but act as if you believe it. It will work. I guarantee it!

As you explore and grow and learn through your explorations you may decide to revise your goals. Great! No problem. The part of you that knows will guide you.

♥   Throughout this process, make regular entries (at lease once a week) in your journal. What are you learning, relearning, and/or becoming aware of?

♥   Throughout this process, continue to meet regularly with your prosperity partner(s). Share with them what you are learning along the way.

♥   Throughout this process, continue to create rewards and celebrations for yourself as you reach significant milestones. Document them in your journal.

Continue to monitor your thoughts and words and be conscious to choose the thoughts and words that will create success. Continue to practice gratitude for the blessings and the challenges of each day. Continue to practice the law of circulation — giving generously of your time, talents, love, and money. Continue to forgive and to forgive and to forgive — yourself and others — until you understand, truly, that there is nothing to forgive.

There is absolutely no limit to what you can be, do, or have as you continue this process, except of course the limits you place on yourself.

A final note: In my life, I have found it helpful to clarify for myself what I want and at the same time to practice detachment. For me, this means that I decide what I want, I ask the Universe to support me in receiving it, and I take the steps I can take toward manifesting that desire. All the time I'm doing this, I expect "this or something better." I realize that my human understanding, wisdom, and/or insight is finite. I know there could be a better plan for me — better than anything I might imagine. So, I always maintain the attitude that "I want what I want" AND "I am willing to receive something better!"

Another aspect of detachment is this: I have decided I will not let my serenity or joy or gratitude be determined by my having or not having any material thing. So...

I want what I want,
I deserve to have what I want,
I will NOT settle for less,
I am willing to receive what I want
OR something better,
I am willing to take the steps
I can take to manifest what I want,
AND
I will be happy and peaceful and grateful
no matter what.

This may sound like a cop-out. I assure you, it is not. **Today I enjoy having everything I truly want AND SO CAN YOU!**

Most important, I enjoy the journey. As Jacqueline Small says, "The journey is where it's AT!" All of this stuff in the material world is fun, it's pleasurable, it's definitely a blessing, but we know that it is temporary. **The lessons we learn as spiritual beings on a human journey are eternal!**

Affirmations

I set specific goals and let the Universe lead me to accomplish them in perfect order.

I attract to me all of the people, information, and resources I need in order to manifest everything that I want.

I am rich, well and happy and every phase of my life is in order now.*

Vast improvement comes quickly in every phase of my life now.*

I use the positive power of the Universe with wisdom, love, and good judgment in handling all of my affairs now.*

I dissolve in my own mind, and in the minds of all others, any idea that my own can be withheld from me. No person, thing, or event can keep that from me which the Universe has for me now.*

I am free, rich, and financially independent now.*

I am receiving all the wealth that the Universe has for me now.*

I give thanks for the immediate complete payment of all financial obligations now, quickly, easily, and in peace.*

I now move forward into my expanded good divinely directed and lavishly prospered.*

I am now guided into my true place with the true people and the true prosperity I deserve — quickly, easily and in peace. I now come into an innumerable company of angels.*

(adapted from the writings of Catherine Ponder, Palm Desert, California, 1971)*

From My Prosperity Scrapbook

"If you don't know where you're going, you'll end up somewhere else."

— *Yogi Berra*

"Take into account that great love and great achievements involve great risk."

— *His Holiness the Dalai Lama*

"Our deepest fear is not that we are inadequate. Our deepest fear is that we are powerful beyond measure. It is our light, not our darkness, that most frightens us. We ask ourselves, who am I to be brilliant, gorgeous, talented, and fabulous?

Actually, who are you not to be?

You are a child of God. Your playing small doesn't serve the world. There's nothing enlightened about shrinking so that other people won't feel insecure around you. We are born to manifest the glory of God that is within us. It's not just in some of us; it's in everyone. And as we let our own light shine, we unconsciously give other people permission to do the same. As we are liberated from our own fear, our presence automatically liberates others."

— *Marianne Williamson*

Jacqueline McMakin is the director of the nonprofit organization called Working from the Heart *and co-author of the book* Working from the Heart. *She advises:*

"Ask yourself, 'How can I do what I love and make X amount of money at it?' It's a crucial mindset change, to take your obstacles and turn them into learning goals. Then, network to find the answers you need ... ask everyone you meet if they have any ideas how you can accomplish that goal. You never know where you'll find the answers you need. The key is focusing your attention on manifesting your dream rather than feeling stuck and miserable about your situation and why you can't reach or pursue that dream."

What the Bible Says About It...

Delight yourself also in the Lord, and He will give you the desires and secret petitions of your heart. Commit your way to the Lord (roll and repose each care of your load on Him); trust (lean on, rely on, and be confident) also in Him and He will bring it to pass. **Psalm 37:4,5 AB**

And all things, whatsoever ye shall ask in prayer, believing, ye shall receive. **Matthew 21:22 KJV**

I tell you, therefore, whatever you ask in prayer, believe that you have received it and it will be yours. **Mark 11:24 MLB**

And I tell you, Ask, and it will be given you; seek, and you will find; knock, and it will be opened to you. **Luke 11:9 RSV**

Yes, ask anything, using my name, and I will do it. **John 14:14 LB**

If ye abide in me, and my words abide in you, ye shall ask what ye will, and it shall be done unto you. **John 15:7 KJV**

Do not fret or have any anxiety about anything, but in every circumstance and in everything, by prayer and petition (definite requests), with thanksgiving, continue to make your wants known to God. **Philippians 4:6 AB**

I have learned how to get along happily whether I have much or little. I know how to live on almost nothing or with everything. I have learned the secret of contentment in every situation, whether it be a full stomach or hunger, plenty or want; for I can do everything God asks me to with the help of Christ who gives me the strength and power. **Philippians 4:11-13 LB**

Abbreviations:
AB = Amplified Bible
KJV = King James Version
LB = Living Bible
MLB = Modern Language Bible
RSV = Revised Standard Version
RSV = Revised Standard Version

Chapter 7: The Power of Financial Literacy
Making Money Work For You

"I serve God. Money serves me."
— Edwene Gaines

If you have followed the suggestions offered in this workbook in the previous chapters, I expect you now have, or soon will have, an increase of cash flowing into your life. Assuming this, I want to offer you a bonus chapter on what to do with some of that cash — after you have tithed, of course! But first, a little more of my own story.

Several years ago when I decided to attract my ideal spiritual partner, I created a long list of qualities and characteristics I would like to have in that partner. I then released my desire to the Universe and asked for "this or something better." Well, I got everything I asked for and MORE! The Universe, in its infinite wisdom, sent me a partner who not only met all the criteria I had asked for but also knew how to make money work for him. Unlike me, he had been systematically saving and investing money for many years. (If you don't think that's an absolute miracle, I could tell you about my last husband!)

When we met, I was almost forty years old, had a master's degree, had professional credentials and licenses, had owned my own business for many years, had earned lots of money, and had spent all that I earned! And I had spent most of it on things that lost value significantly as soon as I paid for them. I was financially illiterate. The Universe knew I needed someone to help me learn to make money work for me!

Now, there are other ways to become financially literate. This is simply the way the Universe and I decided I would begin to be educated in these matters. I find it quite convenient.

Without financial literacy, I generated a great deal of income but had no clue as to how to effectively manage the assets for my best good. Do you remember the second *Rocky* movie? Rocky had won the big fight and now had LOTS of money, which he proceeded to spend on things like cars, clothes, and expensive jewelry. Soon he was flat broke again.

We see this phenomenon in real life with lottery winners. Just recently I heard that approximately one-third of lottery winners declare bankruptcy within a few years of winning big.

As I write this, Jim and I have been together for seven years. Being in partnership with this awesome man has taught me many things. (I think he would agree he has also learned a few things through me!)

The things I understand today about financial literacy I have learned from him and from some limited reading. My purpose in this chapter is just to get you to thinking and to encourage you to pursue your financial education with other teachers.

Basically, what I know about financial management can be summarized in this way:

#1. Money spent on consumer goods is money devalued. Consumer goods immediately lose monetary value when they are purchased. If the consumer goods are charged on a credit card and are not paid off with the first statement, the interest and fees charged increase the loss of value.

This is not to imply that no money should ever be spent on consumer goods. This is to ask the question, "How much is enough?" In our materialistic culture, the typical answer is, "No amount is ever enough." No matter how much "stuff" we have, we are programmed by the advertising media to think that we need more and more and more. We are programmed to believe that when we acquire the "right stuff" we will be happy. Of course, it's a lie, but if we don't know what else to do, we keep buying newer, bigger, supposedly better stuff — even if we have to go into debt to acquire it.

Someone said, **"You can never get enough of what you don't want."** What I think this means is this: What we really want is to feel loved, to feel valuable, and to feel a sense of meaning and purpose in our lives. If we are expecting material things to make us feel good, to make us feel lovable, to make us feel important, we can never get enough. It just doesn't work.

I mentioned previously that Jim and I choose to live simply. We enjoy the things we purchase. It just seems that the longer we practice prosperity principles, the less we want to buy. Beyond a reasonable level of comfort and convenience, we are quite content.

Like us, you may find that as you grow spiritually, you use or consume less and enjoy it more!

I remember the first time my spiritual teacher told me to write down my list of things I want. On that first list was "gold and diamond jewelry." Within a relatively short time I had diamond rings on both my hands, gold chains, and other expensive pieces of jewelry. I enjoyed them greatly at the time. Gradually, over the years, jewelry has become less and less important to me. I have lost or given away all of my rings except one — a rather modest diamond ring that I consider my wedding ring. I wear it only on special occasions.

If I had it to do over, knowing what I know now, some of the money that I exchanged for jewelry would have been saved and invested. That money would still be working for me by earning interest and dividends.

Whatever is on your list, I encourage you to go for it! I support you 100 percent without condition. If you want diamond rings on all of your fingers and half your toes — go for it! And enjoy it!

And I encourage you to know that there are some things money will not buy.

#2. Regular saving and investing is appropriate and wise. DON'T save money for a rainy day or for a medical emergency or for any reason motivated by fear. Save money so it can work for you by earning you interest! Remember always **one of the basic tenets of prosperity is "Money works for me!"** Money is a wonderful servant and a terrible master.

I have made several references to our materialistic, secular culture. Living in this culture is a challenge and a blessing. One of the blessings is that we have created an economic system whereby ANYONE can become wealthy and financially independent, which can be defined as the situation in which a person's money is earning so much money for them that the person does not ever have to work for money to pay their living expenses.

Money is a wonderful servant and a terrible master.

In our culture, there is no caste system that decides a child's fate before it is born. Today, in the United States, anyone with average intelligence and physical health can acquire financial resources and invest them in such a way that the money earns money for that investor. If the investor contributes systematically to his/her savings plan over a certain period of time, the compounded interest alone on that savings principle can amount to more than the investor might ever earn in salaries, wages, commissions, or contract fees in a lifetime.

It is reported that Albert Einstein once said that "compound interest is the greatest power in the Universe."

I shared in a previous chapter that my husband Jim and I now hold financial assets to the extent that we never have to earn another penny and can continue to live at our present standard of living or better until we are 100 years old and can still expect to have money left in our estate. I will share with you now that only about 10 to 12 percent of those assets is money that one of us actually earned in salaries. The rest is interest and dividends paid on investments and compounded over a relatively short period of time — approximately 15 years. (By the way, it is truly phenomenal how those assets began to grow when we started tithing on them!)

Another blessing of our culture is that it is now very common for employers to provide benefits to their employees in the form of 401K and 403B programs. With these programs the employer actually matches money that the employee saves up to a certain percentage of the employee's income. What a deal! Ironically, many employees do not take advantage of such benefits. All of their paychecks are being spent paying interest on credit cards for things they can't even remember buying!

If you have not done so already, I challenge you to begin to consider this question, "How can I make money work for me?"

#3. Money wisely invested in the stock market can work much more efficiently for me than money invested in so-called safer ways. Traditional thought is that investing in the stock market is too risky for the average person. Don't believe it! According to the Vanguard Group, a company which sells mutual funds, the average annual return on money invested in the stock market between 1926 and 1999 was 11.3 percent. This rate of return is much higher than the nominal rate of interest paid on passbook savings accounts, money market accounts, or treasury bills.

There is a great deal of media attention being paid to people who are making and losing huge fortunes in the stock market. There is less media attention given to people who just quietly continue, month after month, year after year, to build financial assets that eventually equal financial independence.

This chapter of the workbook does not include any required writing — just some suggestions.

If you have not done so already, begin to read and talk to people and do whatever you can to become financially literate — to understand how our economic system works and how you can make it work for you. Information is easily available. You can start by reading the financial section of your newspaper, if you don't do that already. You can read the *Wall Street Journal*. You can watch "Wall Street Week" on Friday nights on PBS. The bookstores are full of books that can help you get started. (An excellent book that Jim and I both enjoyed and recommend is *Rich Dad, Poor Dad: What the Rich Teach Their Kids About Money — That the Poor and Middle Class Do Not!*)

Do you know people who invest in the stock market with good results? If so, ask them how they got started. Ask them how they decide where to invest. Community colleges often offer introductory courses on investing for a nominal registration fee. If your employer offers a savings and investment plan, talk with the benefits coordinator and find out everything he or she can tell you about the benefit available to you there.

One word of caution: Do not trust everything a financial services professional might tell you. Get several opinions. Many financial services professionals are honest people with integrity who are following their bliss and who are sincerely committed to the best interests of their clients. Some, however, are just trying to pay the minimum balance on this month's credit card bill! If you do decide to use the services of a financial professional, interview several before choosing one and ask the Universe to send you to the right person. Let your inner wisdom guide you to that person.

Also, be aware that my partner Jim Auxier is available to be your prosperity coach. Jim has a bachelor's degree in Business and a master's degree in Administrative Science. At one time he was a licensed broker of financial services. His expertise is primarily in the areas of personal money management, financial goal-setting, saving and investment strategies, freedom from debt, and lifestyle issues affecting prosperity. He no longer sells financial services of any kind, but he is available to give you some general guidance in the areas mentioned. You can reach him by leaving a message at this toll-free voice mail number: 1-866-633-6954. or you can send e-mail to him at jim@prosperity-park.com. His coaching services are offered in exchange for a free-will donation.

You might be thinking, what does all of this stuff about investing in the stock market have to do with spiritual principles? Here is my only answer to that — as spiritual beings on a human journey, it's all spiritual! Learning to make money work for us can be a self-empowerment process in itself. It can free us to follow our bliss and serve the world in ways that would never be possible if we spend a significant portion of our time working for money and paying interest on consumer debt.

So, you now have just about everything I know about financial literacy. I know a lot more than I used to know and I'm learning all the time!

FROM MY PROSPERITY SCRAPBOOK

Just A Dime

Can one dime make a difference? Here is a woman who turned a dime into millions of dollars.

Her name was Martha Berry. This clever woman founded the Berry School in Rome, Georgia. She scraped together funds from every source possible. One day she approached Henry Ford, of Ford automobile fame, and asked for a contribution. Patronizingly, he reached into his pocket and pulled out a dime.

Rather than be insulted or discouraged by the "gift," Miss Berry bought a package of seed peanuts with it. The seeds were planted and tended, and they eventually yielded a large crop which she later sold.

Again she called on Mr. Ford. "Here's the dime you gave me last year," she said, handing him a coin. Then she told him of the return she had realized from his token investment.

Ford was so impressed that, in the years to come, he gave millions of dollars to the school.

Can one dime make a difference? Yes, if we invest it well.

How about one hour of your time? Can it make a difference? Or how about the life of one person? Can a life like yours or mine REALLY make a difference? The answer to each of these questions is the same. Yes, if we invest it well.

Now... how are your investments doing?

— Author Unknown

What the Bible Says About It...

Again, the Kingdom of Heaven can be illustrated by the story of a man going into another country, who called together his servants and loaned them money to invest for him while he was gone.

He gave $5,000 to one, $2,000 to another, and $1,000 to the last — dividing it in proportion to their abilities — and then left on his trip. The man who received the $5,000 began immediately to buy and sell with it and soon earned another $5,000. The man with $2,000 went right to work, too, and earned another $2,000.

But the man who received the $1,000 dug a hole in the ground and hid the money for safekeeping.

After a long time their master returned from his trip and called them to him to account for his money. The man to whom he had entrusted the $5,000 brought him $10,000.

His master praised him for good work. "You have been faithful in handling this small amount," he told him, "so now I will give you many more responsibilities. Begin the joyous tasks I have assigned to you."

Next came the man who had received the $2,000, with the report, "Sir, you gave me $2,000 to use, and I have doubled it."

"Good work," his master said. "You are a good and faithful servant. You have been faithful over this small amount, so now I will give you much more."

Then the man with the $1,000 came and said, "Sir, I knew you were a hard man, and I was afraid you would rob me of what I earned, so I hid your money in the earth and here it is!"

But his master replied, "Wicked man! Lazy slave! Since you knew I would demand your profit, you should at least have put my money into the bank so I could have some interest. Take the money from this man and give it to the man with the $10,000. For the man who uses well what he is given shall be given more, and he shall have abundance. But from the man who is unfaithful, even what little responsibility he has shall be taken from him."

Matthew 25: 14 - 29 (Living Bible)

Conclusion

Eastern wisdom says, "When the student is ready, the teacher appears." If this notebook has been of any use or value to you, it is because you were ready to hear and live the Truth.

Writing this workbook has been a great blessing to me — in writing it I am following my bliss! I am compelled by my inner wisdom to do this and I have followed that guidance trusting that the Universe will bless this effort.

Mother Teresa once said, "There are no great acts. There are only small acts performed with great love." I like to think that this workbook is a small act performed with great love. My conscious intention has been to express love and unconditional support to all who use it.

Whatever your experiences with this workbook, I would love to hear from you! My desire is to be an ongoing partner, cheerleader, and coach for you if that would be helpful to you. I am available for consultation by e-mail or through "snail mail." If my consultation is helpful to you, I will invite you to send me a donation. This is to support your prosperity — by giving back you will keep the good blessings flowing in your direction! (You can determine the amount of the donation within a suggested range.)

I would also appreciate hearing how this workbook could be improved — how could it be revised to be more useful and helpful? If you have any suggestions, please let me know. Also, let me know what is particularly meaningful or beneficial to you in this workbook.

I encourage you to continue to set your goals and to go for it, to journal, and to meet with and share with your prosperity partner(s). Remember that the Universe loves and supports you without condition. Whatever challenges you face as you manifest your prosperity are learning experiences that you have attracted and created for your own evolution.

Whatever you do, don't ever give up! Jesus, the master teacher, said, **"Keep on asking and it will be given you; keep on seeking and you will find; keep on knocking (reverently) and the door will be opened. For everyone who keeps on asking receives; and he who keeps on seeking finds; and to him who keeps on knocking, the door will be opened." Matthew 7:7-8 (Amplified Bible)**

In the Eastern world, many people greet and leave one another with the word "Namaste" (pronounced nuh MOS tay). It means that the Divine within me recognizes, honors, and salutes or "waves to" the Divine that is within you. So I conclude with the word "Namaste!"

Epilogue

I offer you one final gift from my prosperity scrapbook. This is something that I clipped and saved from a church newsletter. It is a version of the prayer that is commonly known as The Lord's Prayer. *According to the gospels, this is the prayer that Jesus taught his disciples. Bible scholars over the centuries have translated the prayer into English according to their best understanding and insight at that time. More recent scholarship into the ancient Aramaic language of Jesus' day has revealed a prayer that is the very essence of prosperity consciousness. I share it with you now as my prayer for your richest blessings, peace, joy, and prosperity.*

The Prayer of Jesus
(A Direct Translation From Aramaic To English)

Cosmic Birther of all radiance and vibration —

soften the ground of our being and carve out a space within us
where Your presence can abide.

Fill us with your creativity so that we may be empowered
to bear the fruit of Your mission.

Let each of our actions bear fruit in accordance with our desire.

Endow us with the wisdom to produce and share
what each being needs to grow and flourish.

Untie the tangled threads of destiny that bind us
as we release others from the entanglement of past mistakes.

Do not let us be seduced by that which would divert us from our true purpose,
but illuminate the opportunities of the present moment.

For you are the ground and the fruitful vision, the birth-power and fulfillment,
as all is gathered and made whole once again.

Appendix I

Creating Your Prosperity Group

Working with a small group of prosperity partners can make an enormous difference in your degree of success and in the pace at which you achieve your success. Spiritual beings on a human journey were never intended to make the journey alone. Here are a few guidelines and suggestions for you to consider as you recruit and covenant with your prosperity group.

Decide on one or two meeting days and times that would work well for you. As you approach people about being a part of the group, let them know what days and times you have in mind.

As you recruit, let people know that you are looking for partners who will commit to attending a weekly meeting unless there is an unavoidable conflict. Also let them know that each group member will agree to do work in the workbook each week between meetings. Each person can move at his/her own pace, as long as they are willing to do SOMETHING each week between meetings. Let people know that you are looking for partners who are seriously ready to start making changes to create prosperity in their lives.

The ideal meeting space may be a "neutral" public place if there is a convenient space available at little or no cost. If the meeting is held in someone's home, I would recommend that different homes be used each week. Ideally, distractions such as phones and pagers will be minimized.

When you have four to six people who are ready to begin, schedule your first meeting. Each person needs to have his or her own workbook by the first group meeting.

At your first meeting you can decide how each meeting will begin. I recommend that leadership in the group rotate each meeting. The volunteer convener (or servant leader) can call the group to order.

I highly recommend that you start on time each week with whoever is present. You may find that there are people who are habitually late, and if you make a practice of starting late to accommodate that person, you will encourage others to come late also.

There will be times when there are unavoidable delays that cause people to be late. When someone comes in late, there is no reason for shaming or rescuing. The person arriving late can slip quietly into the group and enjoy the rest of it. Group members who are already present need feel no obligation to recap for the late-comer what has already been discussed.

Agree together at the first meeting that you will honor confidentiality within the group. This is vitally important to the safety and effectiveness of the group. This simply means that what is said in the group stays in the group. Group members are free to share with others outside the group anything they themselves may have learned or realized during the group. But everyone is asked to commit to keeping the group trust by NOT repeating personal information that is shared within the context of the group.

Also, agree to observe the "no gossip" rule — have an understanding that between meetings two or more group members will not discuss others in the group in a way that you would not want the others to overhear.

You may want to start each meeting with a moment of silence, a brief check-in from each member, an affirmation by each group member, or by lighting a candle. If you allow time for a check-in, I recommend that your volunteer leader for each week use a timer set for one or two minutes. When the timer sounds, the person who is checking in is asked to wrap up and pass to the next person.

I highly recommend that the time in the group be focused on sharing exercises completed in the workbook. Staying focused is essential to manifesting prosperity, and staying focused within the group is excellent practice.

To help maintain this focus, it may be best to keep any eating or drinking during the group to a minimum. Your group may want to occasionally plan a meal or other social occasion together. No problem at all! But let that time be in addition to your regular meeting.

The ideal time limit for the group may be 90 minutes. One hour can also be effective if the group has no more than three or four members. For four to six members, 90 minutes will work better. Longer than 90 minutes may be too long.

Your group members can agree together how long the meeting will last each week. Again, you may want to agree on a way to end the group each week — with a prayer, an affirmation, a moment of silence, or by extinguishing the candle. Having your volunteer convener lead a simple opening and closing ritual will help to create the space for the group.

The servant leader can also ask near the beginning of the meeting, "Who has something from your workbook or journal that you are ready to share?" There may be one or more people who *could* share and one or more who feel an *urgent need* to share. Determine which group members feel an urgent need to share. Assume that there is plenty of time for everyone's needs to be addressed, and agree that together you will create that reality.

As each person shares from their workbook and/or journal, he or she can decide whether or not to ask for feedback from the rest of the group. The person sharing may prefer to hear *only* affirmations in response to their sharing. Group members need give feedback only when it is specifically requested.

Remember, feedback is not advice. *Avoid giving advice.* Advice-giving assumes a "one up" position and assumes that the person being advised is not capable of making discoveries and decisions for themselves.

Instead, give feedback in the form of statements such as, "This is what I am hearing you say," or "This is what I see," or "This is how I can relate to what you are sharing," or "This is my concern or wish for you." In offering feedback, use the principle of *honesty with love.* Honesty without love is brutality. Love without honesty is sentimentality.

Let each person take responsibility for asking for what he or she wants from the group. There is no need for mind-reading.

This is not a therapy group. If any person in the group is experiencing serious emotional challenges (for example, serious depression or anxiety or acute grief reactions) that person may need to be using the services of a mental health professional. A person with these challenges may still be an effective member of a prosperity partners group. However, *the entire group needs to stay focused on the issues addressed in the workbook.*

The group can decide at or before the first meeting whether the commitment to meet is indefinite (open-ended) or time-limited. For example, the first commitment the group members make may be for 12 weeks. At the end of 12 weeks the group members can decide whether or not they want to continue and whether or not they want to invite new members to join.

If someone decides that they want to leave the group before the initial commitment has been met, bless them and let them go. If someone's leaving brings up abandonment issues, let the person who is feeling abandoned write about that in his or her journal and do affirmation work to address that issue.

New members can be a great asset to the group if everyone is comfortable with the idea of inviting new people to join at certain intervals. One or more new persons can join the group and start at the beginning of the workbook even though other members may be farther along in the process. If a new person joins take a few minutes at the beginning of the new person's first meeting to review the group guidelines of confidentiality, no gossip, starting and ending on time, feedback instead of advice, and so on. (See the summary list of guiding principles at the end of this appendix).

Remember that the purpose of being in the group together is to give one another unconditional support and to act as witnesses and companions for one another on the spiritual journey. Each group member can also choose to hold themselves accountable to the group. This is very different from the group holding its members accountable. Each group member is ultimately responsible for himself or herself.

Remember that *you are all students and you are all teachers.* Everyone has something valuable and important to contribute. As spiritual beings on a human journey everyone is equal, whatever your previous experience or lack of experience with these or other spiritual principles. Do not sabotage yourself with negative comparisons to other group members.

Every group member is your mirror. If you see anything positive or admirable in other group members, remember that "what you see is what you are." You could not recognize positive traits in others if that trait were not also present within you. Also, if there is something irritating or unattractive about a group member, remember that "what you see is what you are." You could not recognize *any* trait, positive or negative, in another person if it were not also present to some degree within you!

Be grateful to each and every group member who journeys with you. The ones who sometimes irritate you can be your greatest and most profound teachers.

In summary, then, keep in mind the suggested principles for conducting a group, listed on the next page.

Principles for Conducting a Group:

Neutral location

Rotating leadership

Starting and ending on time

Regular attendance
(always be there unless there is an unavoidable conflict)

Commitment to the process
(doing work between group meetings)

Confidentiality

No gossip

Maintain focus on the workbook

Give feedback instead of advice

Honesty with love

Sharing time, knowing that there is plenty of time

Self-responsibility

Unconditional support

Equality

Gratitude for mirrors

Remember, you do not have to do this perfectly. Being in the group is a learning process for everyone. If there are issues that arise that I may be able to help with, contact me and I will be happy to offer any assistance that I can.

Know that you are on a fantastic journey of discovery. I applaud you, I celebrate you, I support you 100 percent without condition.

Appendix 2: About Your Guarantee

If you have completed this workbook as instructed and are not completely satisfied with the results, you may return it for a full refund of the purchase price.

Return the completed workbook and a copy of your journal. You are not required to send a copy of the inventory work assigned in chapter 4.

Send your materials to:
Grace Terry
779 E. Merritt Island Causeway, #1351
Merritt Island, FL 32952

Please be sure to include your name and mailing address. Allow four to six weeks for your refund.

Also, if you would like a personal contact from the author, include your phone number, the best time to call, and/or your e-mail address.

On the other hand, if you have been greatly blessed by this workbook — far beyond what you expected when you bought it — if you would like to give something back and keep the good flowing into your life, you may want to consider sending us an extra donation. We will accept it with gratitude, knowing that you will be blessed by your giving, and will use your donation to continue to share these teachings with others.

Blessings to you!

About the Author

Grace Terry, MSW, has been making a positive difference for more than 20 years. For many of those years she was a licensed mental health professional in a successful private practice. She received her Master of Social Work degree in 1980. She is now a full-time workshop/retreat/seminar leader, sacred storyteller, wellness and prosperity coach, prosperity teacher, mentor, journalist, and author. Grace is the co-creator of "The Awakened Woman Network."

Also Available from Grace Terry, MSW

A Woman's Pathway to Peace, Power, and Prosperity, a two-and-one-half hour audio taped workshop, is an excellent companion to the *Prosperity Guaranteed* workbook.

In this dynamic workshop, Grace Terry discusses the inherent spiritual power of all women, the ways feminine power may be unconsciously discounted, drained or given away, and ways that women can reclaim their spiritual power and use it to create a life of joy and abundance.

To receive your professionally recorded, edited, and packaged tape set in a deluxe album, visit our web-site at www.prosperity-park.com or call toll free 1-866-633-6954.

Do you find yourself repeating self-defeating patterns in your relationships? Does your heart long for a true spiritual partnership? *Attracting and Maintaining An Ideal Spiritual Partnership* is another audio taped workshop based on the principles of the *Prosperity Guaranteed* workbook. In this workshop, Grace Terry discusses the inner dynamics that influence our outer relationships. Whether you are single or committed to a long-term relationship, this enlightening two-hour workshop will help you create and sustain a joyful, loving partnership that works!

To receive your professionally recorded, edited, and packaged tape set in a deluxe album, visit our web-site at www.prosperity-park.com or call toll free 1-866-633-6954.

The *Prosperity Guaranteed* workbook is also available as an E-book downloaded from our website in pdf format. You can then open the file with Adobe Acrobat to read at your leisure and/or print a working hard-copy.

For more information, visit our web-site at www.prosperity-park.com or contact Grace Terry, at terrytraveling@aol.com or toll free voice mail 1-866-633-6954.